ACADEMIC LEADERSHIP

*Practical Wisdom for
Deans and Administrators*

ISRAEL GALINDO

Academic Leadership: Practical Wisdom for Deans and Administrators
Copyright © 2020, Israel Galindo
All rights reserved.

No part of this publication may be reproduced, stored in a retrieval system, or transmitted in any form or by any other means, electronic, mechanical, photocopying, recording, or otherwise, without the prior permission of the copyright owner, except for brief quotations included in a review of the book.

Acknowledgements: portions of this book were previously published in the Blog for Theological School Deans of the Wabash Center for Teaching and Learning in Religion and Theology. Reprinted with permission.

Published by Didache Press
Decatur, GA

Acknowledgements

I want to express appreciation to the Wabash Center for Teaching and Learning in Theology and Religion for permission to re-print portions of this book. Many chapters have appeared in the Center's blogs. The author also thanks the members of the 2013 Colloquy for Theological School Deans, co-led with Dr. Rebecca Slough and with Harold Washington, Michael DeLashmutt, Paul Chilcote, Justus Baird, Tom Pearson, Morrey Davis, Ron Feenstra, Sue Garrett, Steve Peay, Sarah Drummond, and Sang-Ehil Han. It remains among the most fruitful and meaningful professional development experiences in over twenty years of higher education. Particular appreciation is expressed to Dr. Lynn Westfield, Director, and Dr. Paul Myhre, Senior Associate Director of the Wabash Center, and their outstanding staff, for their many kindnesses and considerations.

Israel Galindo
Decatur, GA

CONTENTS

INTRODUCTION 1

I. ACADEMIC LEADERSHIP

You Probably Should Not Be a Dean If 7
Six Challenges When Taking the Job of Dean 11
The Deanship as Vocation 16
Eight Challenges You WILL Face as Dean 20
Four Blind Spots Every Dean Needs to Avoid 25
Paradoxes of Educational Leadership 29
Four Freaking Awesome Things About
Being a Dean 33
Fixing the Problems of Higher Education 37
Physics for Deans 42
Leadership Secrets of Effective Deans 47
Nine Ways to Dean Like a Pirate 49
Five Essential Functions of the Dean 52
The Political Dean 55
How Academic Institutions Stay Stuck 59
The Dean in the Age of Change 61
The Dean Creates the Right Kind of Change 65
The Dean and Cultural Change 67
The Dean and Organizational Change 69
20 Ways the Dean Can Say "No" 71
When Faculty Members Misbehave 72
Deaning From the Right Side of the Brain 77
The Dean as Positive Deviant 82
Leading from the Center 84

Everything Takes Five Years 87
The Nine Best Ways to Ruin Your Staff 89
Six Challenges When Leaving the Office 95

II. ACADEMIC ADMINISTRATION

The Dean and Assessment 100
The Dean and Educational Effectiveness 102
The Dean and Educational Fundamentals 105
Eight Big Ideas About Assessment 107
Educational Concepts Every Dean Needs to Know .. 110
Creating a High Impact Curriculum 113
What Matters is a 21st Century Curriculum? 116
The Dean and Program Risk Assessment 120
Starting a New Degree Program is the Last
Thing a Dean Should Do 124
The Dean as Problem-Solver 127
The Dean and Wicked Problems 130
Six Types of Assessment Every Dean Needs 133
Using Grade Distribution Reports 136
Using Program-Level Assessment Rubrics 139

Appendix 146
Bibliography 150

Introduction

Sometimes, when someone takes on a new administrative role in an organization I say, "Welcome to the other side of the desk." Going from a staff or teaching position to that of administration will change one's perspective. This is merely the result of changing one's position in the system. That move demands a different way of functioning within the system with different priorities that come with the job. When a faculty member becomes a dean it does not take long before one may hear someone say, "You know, you've changed since becoming dean" (intended as a compliment or criticism!).

There are what I believe to be pedagogies of context and position that shape our frames of references, perceptions, and ways of knowing. That is, one's context and position in an organization shapes the way one thinks. The dynamics of these pedagogies have to do with the epidemiologies of practice. For example, these pedagogies are iterative (they involve patterns of thinking and practice) and heuristic (they involve perpetual problem solving). These two dynamics alone, over time, shape our ability to "think like a dean."

Pedagogies of Context

We tend to under appreciate and underestimate the power of context in learning. In a recent conversation I once again heard the sentiment that we need to keep our students in school longer to better prepare them for the professional workplace. What may tend to be unrealized is that keeping students longer in a context that keeps them in the role of "student," dependent on others for expertise, and experiencing themselves as novices rather than leaders, merely reinforces their formation as *students*. To put it bluntly, you learn to do what you do, and not something else. If you want to learn how to lead and organization, then you need to actually be in a position of leadership in an organization, not study about leading. If you really want to learn engineering, practice engineering in the field it is applied.

The situated context of a school frames the "character" of both the office and person of the dean. The imperatives of an institution whose mission is in support of education and the particular corporate ethos of a faculty whose cognates are biased toward their academic guilds require practices in the function of the dean that shapes both the dean and the organization. To put it another way, the context of a school calls out dimensions of the work of the dean in that school to the extent it is unique in higher education.

Pedagogies of Position

Deans occupy a unique position in schools. They learn to think more globally, strategically, and administratively than others in the organization. Their position is that of a Second Chair leader, meaning that while they hold relatively little authority, their sphere of influence can be broad and significant. While the position of dean is that of chief academic administrator they quickly learn that logical and necessary attention to policies, procedures, and protocols can only influence the system so far. Effective deans, then, learn the pedagogy of relationships of their particular organizational cultures that help to actually bring about change. Few in the organization, aside from the dean, are in the position to tap into those facets of influence.

Having a philosophical framework that informs practice, decisions (not only what is decided, but how one goes about it), and function is vital to the role of academic leader. Demonstrating integrity, extending grace, being redemptive in relationships, are as critical to the health, vitality and effectiveness of the position and work of dean as is administrative competence.

Thinking Like a Dean

It takes about three years to learn the job of dean, and about four years to achieve competence. Eventually, the pedagogy of context and position will help us think like a dean. What might that look like? Below are some examples.

- You learn to appreciate that your priority is the welfare of the organization and not particularly that of individuals in the organization
- You are aware that you sit at the tension point of numerous anxious triangle (the faculty-the president-the board)
- Your priorities of focus change. For me, it is "The curriculum first, the needs of the student second, personal preferences, predilections and peccadilloes third" (previously it may have been, my scholarship, my teaching, my students).
- You get clear that you are responsible for your own functioning and not that of others.
- You also must live into the reality that your functioning is not dependent on other people's functioning. (Just because your faculty does not want to practice curriculum assessment does not mean you can stop making it happen)
- You get clear that what people want and what people need are not always equivalent. Give people what they need.
- You become aware that education is situated in the field of higher education. You need to think like an educator as well as a scholar
- You begin to appreciate that the deanship is its own vocation. Too many of us spend a lot of time fretting about not being perceived as scholars in our fields. On this job, something has to give, or, as my mother reminded her children, "You can have anything you want, but you cant' have everything you want." While you are dean, invest in the scholarship of the deanship.

- You become aware that a part of the job is fighting against inertia in order to make progress. Rare are the faculty and program leaders who characteristically demonstrate initiative in developing, refining, improving, or enhancing the curriculum or programs. Those perspectives and initiatives seem to be "assigned" to the dean. Unless you initiate and push for progress, it likely will not happen.

Doing the work of the dean, or that of an educational administrator, changes the way one thinks about education, teaching and learning, students and faculty. So, when someone tells you, "You've changed since you became dean," just say, "Yes, thank you for noticing."

I. ACADEMIC LEADERSHIP

You Probably Should Not Be a Dean If…

Deans often come from the Faculty, for a variety of reasons. Sometimes it's a question of who is most willing to serve (or, who missed the meeting when the vote was taken!). Sometimes it's a decision based of budget constraints. Sometimes it's political. More often than not, it is a well-intentioned and properly motivated response to the need of the school for someone to serve in that capacity. Good intentions and high ideals are a good start, but, sadly, not sufficient to meet the demands of the job and function of the deanship.

If you, or a colleague, are in the position of deciding whether or not to answer the call to step into the deanship, here's a short list of things to consider when deciding. You probably should not be a dean . . .

If you don't like meetings. Deans lead from the center of the organization. As such, you'll occupy a place in the organization that is connected to just about every other corner of the organization. That will necessitate more meetings than you thought could possibly be scheduled any given week, with committees, groups, students, faculty, vendors, staff, and anyone who wants to make a claim on your time and favor. You can resolve to reduce your attendance at meetings, but the fact is the need for the presence of the dean will not likely allow for much reduction in this activity.

If you have a low tolerance for pain and loneliness. While deans occupy the second chair position in the organization, they still have a key leadership role to play. Anyone who occupies a position of leadership in an organization will deal with pain and loneliness inherent to leadership. Be prepared to weather personal attacks, having your motives questioned, accused of being power-hungry and manipulative, playing favorites, having "gone to the dark side" and any number of other accusations. This has less to do with you and more to do with the office you occupy, but, you'll feel the pain nevertheless.

If you need to be liked. When a professor friend at another school learned that I was about to become dean, he said, "Now the faculty won't like you." To which I responded, "They don't like me now, so that's not a problem." Schools need their deans to be effective, but not necessarily, and not always, liked. Deans are administrators and managers whose primary responsibility of stewardship is the welfare of the institutions. Deans will never be able to make decisions that will make everyone happy.

If you cannot choose vision and the welfare of the institution over personal relationships or alliances. When a faculty member occupies the office of dean, she or he "shifts" position in the system. That includes a shift in how one relates to all other persons in the organization. The function of the dean calls for a commitment to the welfare and advance of the organization--its mission, health, effectiveness, and relevance--over other concerns that may tip to the welfare of individuals at the expense of the organization. Sometimes, deans have to say "No," to friends, fully realizing the personal cost to both, or, to the relationship.

If you are not willing to learn a new professional field. Schools are firmly planted in the field of higher education. Therefore, deans cannot just be scholars in academic disciplines, they must be competent educational leaders. That means becoming competent in educational administration, educational leadership, educational supervision, educational assessment, and educational planning.

If you are not willing to speak the truth, always. As leaders from the center, deans often have the capacity, and obligation, to "see things as they are." Deans are pragmatists and realists who are not well-served by wishful thinking. One prophetic function of academic deans is to speak the truth, to the President, to trustees, to faculty, and to students.

If you cannot discern between reactivity and sabotage. Deans are agents of change in their organizations. While the phrase "People don't like change," if oft-repeated, we consistently underestimate just how hard change is for people. Whenever the dean initiates change, from policy to program to personnel, the first response is reactivity. That's normal and to be expected, and therefore, does not really require a response. But, deans need to discern when reactivity rises to the level of sabotage--that calls for action and response.

If you are prone to focus on people's feelings over holding them accountable. Deans build the health of their organization by introducing and maintaining accountability in the organization. Holding people accountable goes hand in hand with giving people responsibility. Holding someone accountable for their responsibility does not feel good to anyone, but it is necessary. Focusing on (unpleasant) feelings is beside the point.

If you cannot assess, measure, evaluate, and judge. Deans must engage in quality control in order to ensure the integrity of the organization. That's what assessment is all about: "Are we doing what we say we are doing, and how well?" Assessment and evaluation often call for making a judgment--it's helpful to confess that you cannot lead without judging.

If you aren't a problem-solver. There will be seasons when half your days will involve solving other people's problems. The other half will involve solving institutional problems. The problems never end, but effective deans understand that it's so much about the problems, or how many, as much as how you respond and deal with them. Sschools are institutions of a kind--they all have the same problems, but, each dean must solve the problems of her or his own school.

If you cannot be ruthless about boundaries. While it is true that, to some extent, for the dean "Everything is my business," it is also true that not everything is his or her responsibility. Deans must also ensure that institutional boundaries are respected, among and between administration, trustees, staff, employees, students.

So, do you still want to be a dean? Good! Few things will challenge you more in your personal and professional growth. Join the club!

❖

Six Challenges When Taking the Job of Dean

New deans come into the office of Chief Academic Officer in varied ways. Some aspire to the work, others are called, some are pressed into service, and some poor souls are voted in during a missed Faculty meeting. While larger schools often have the luxury of searching and securing a seasoned person for the job, smaller schools may fill the office out of necessity from among the Faculty body. Given how critical the office is to the effectiveness and development of the institution, it is puzzling how haphazard filling the offices of the dean can seem.

Starting the job of dean can be daunting and may leave one with feelings of uncertainty or with performance-anxiety long ago left behind as one grew confident in one's field of study and in teaching. When taking office, especially as a novice, there is reason to be anxious. It's new work, in a new field, in a new organizational position, with new responsibilities, requiring new skills and expertise. It has been pointed out that when we enter these kinds of situations we tend to emotionally regress to feeling like a nine-year-old on the first day of class at a new school.

Regardless of how a dean lands the job, whether by aspiration or expediency, there are common issues to deal with when taking office. Here are six common challenges deans must navigate as they establish themselves in their new role, whether coming from outside the system, or, emerging from among the Faculty.

1. Establishing and cultivating a different relationship with the President. When you shift from faculty member to administration you occupy a different functional position in the system, and that requires a re-alignment in how you relate to persons in the system. For deans, the single most critical functional relationship is with the President. Depending on the President, the dean's new role may be that of confidant, lieutenant, guide and advisor (leading upward), second chair leader, or, scapegoat and third point of reactivity triangles. Entering deans will do well to invest in cultivating a healthy and transparent relationship with the President (e.g., the dean is not the President's secretary!). If there's a singular quality that helps foster a healthy and productive working relationship between President and dean, it is trust. If there is trust between the two key leaders in the organization, they can work through any issue and navigate just about any crisis. Lacking trust, however, not only will the relationship remain stuck, so will the school.

2. Establishing and cultivating a different relationship with the Faculty and Associates. If you come into the office of the dean from among faculty you'll have to re-establish a new relationship with former faculty colleagues. You are now someone anywhere from "first among equals" to one who has "gone to the dark side." As with all leadership positions, it can be helpful to accept that most people in the system will related to you more out of the role you play than with you personally. If you enter from outside the school you'll want to work on establishing your working relationship with the faculty early: expectations, accessibility, and goals (Hint: those should not include being "liked."). If there are associate deans in place you'll need to work on clarifying boundaries, interfaces, and expectations related to the work and to working together.

3. Acquiring new educational expertise. If you enter the dean's office from a field other than education in general, or higher education in particular, you'll need to acquire a new range of educational expertise---quickly. There is now a whole new field about which you now need to be the resident expert: accreditation standards, processes, and requirements; curriculum assessment; curriculum development; assessment of effectiveness in teaching and learning; educational supervision; budgeting and institutional metrics; project planning, etc. There's just no way around it, the job of the dean is educational administration and institutional leadership. In conversations with deans I've heard scholars confess that nothing in their educational or professional experience prepared them to be educational leaders, while also hearing other deans confess that everything they needed to know about educational leadership they learned from training in the field of elementary education. Taking on the job of dean may mean putting your personal scholarly interests and field of study aside for a short tenure, to some extent. Simply put, taking on the deanship is taking on a new professional field.

4. Acquiring new people skills. The contextual relational skills of the dean are very different than those you've cultivated as scholar and classroom instructor. You'll be surprised, perhaps overwhelmed, at how much "pastoral care" you'll provide as dean---for students and for faculty. You'll need to learn to say "no" twice as often as you say "yes," and do so without alienating or unduly disappointing people. You'll need to learn how to set boundaries, and keep them, as well as when extend less grace for lapses, failures, and infractions than you may be comfortable with. If you have not developed a knack for political gamesmanship as a life skill, now is the time to do so; you'll need it to navigate the perpetually triangulated waters of the job as you work with players, constituents, and stakeholders: faculty, administration, staff, students, trustees, and the public.

The most important people skill for a dean to cultivate, however, is closely aligned to the function of academic leadership: getting a disparate group of people to align with an educational vision (often, one they may not fully support) and making it possible for them to work together toward realizing that vision. For deans, that means getting people to pull together on strategies and initiatives that translate and implement the vision (typically articulated by the President). That's no small feat. Recall the often-used phrase about faculty and herding cats.

5. Restructuring and prioritizing life and work. Those who take on the job of dean anticipate they are going to be busier than the usual academic life allows, but they are often take by surprise by how much they underestimate that reality. One of the biggest challenges when taking office is restructuring and prioritizing life and work for the demands of the deanship. This can include:

- Adjusting to longer work hours
- Spending more time spent in the office
- Attending more meetings, each resulting in more work
- Restructuring one's focus, from scholarship to academics; from teaching to administrivia

- Shifting loyalty to the institution over personal relationships
- Letting go of things that are not sustainable in work and lifestyle
- Meeting more often with people you need to and less often with people you want to
- Changing the kinds of professional meetings you attend.

The work of the dean is challenging, at times it can feel overwhelming. But it can be one of the most satisfying professional seasons of one's academic career, despite the challenges. Starting right can make a big difference in how satisfying the work is, and, how effective one can do it.

6. Getting things in order before making progress. It is likely that one thing you'll be dealing with early into your tenure is taking care of issues left undone, or neglected, by your predecessor. If you came up from the Faculty these may be issues you are aware of, and now it's up to you to address them. If you come from outside the institution, the issues may be on a to-do list from a conscientious predecessor, they may come in the form of a litany of complaints from the President or Faculty, or they may be issues you stumble upon by surprise. In one early educational administration job I discovered a file buried in a filing cabinet indicating the previous person had totally neglected to follow up with federal and state compliance issues. No one in the system was aware of it and it re-prioritized my agenda for the first six months in office. In another academic administration I discovered, in a staff meeting, that the previous administration had not initiated the production of the academic catalog! In one job, it was left to me ("the next guy") to deal with troubling and under performing staff and faculty members. While uncomfortable, dismissing three employees and putting one on notice yielded the benefit of "waking up" the system.

There's no one perfect way to start the complex job of the dean. Many of the issues you'll face entering the office will be contextual---unique, to some extent, to your school. Being alert and appreciating the importance of the establishment phase of your tenure can go a long way to making the rest of time in office productive, if not enjoyable.

❖

The Deanship as Vocation

One axiom about vocations is that it takes about three years to learn a job and about four and a half years to get competent at it. It's something I tell my students as a caution about the complex work of leading, administration, and management, accompanied with the admonition that "It's too soon to quit" during those challenging first years of their first professional job. I'll confess it is advice I've reminded myself during the first years of my deanship. The deanship is its own vocation, and it can help to acquire some perspectives about the job. Here are ten insights gained from experience.

1. The job of the Dean involves constantly pushing against inertia. I've worked in four different professional settings in leadership capacities before my tenure as dean. No other organizational culture has been as resistant to change and slow to make necessary adaptations to development as a school, in my experience. In the critical work of organizational development and institutional advancement, the dean becomes a key force in pushing against inertia. Due to the fact that deans lead "from the middle," this stance becomes complex in a school as her or his office intersects with all others. As one dean said, "I sit on every damn committee around here."

2. It is helpful to remember that my functioning is not dependent on other people's functioning. Because deans lead from the center and intersect with most of the other key offices in the school their capacity for bringing about change or merely getting the job done often can be helped or hindered by others in the organization. It is worth remembering that the dean is responsible for the stewardship of his or her office and how he or she carries out that calling. One is not responsible for how others act or function--from the president to faculty to staff to students to trustees. For example, the mere fact that some faculty members may sabotage progress in curricular revision does not determine whether or not the dean needs to see the revision through to its end.

3. A dean will be successful in bringing about change to the extent the organization allows. One of the dean's function is to bring about necessary changes appropriate to the life of the organization during the dean's term. Yet, organizations tend to resist change, even when necessary. Regardless of the level of "push" a dean is comfortable with (seductive collaboration or

Machiavellian strategics) the fact remains that any leader will only be able to bring about the changes the organization allows.

4. As dean you are responsible for your tenure in office, not the previous and not the following. Whether you serve one term or the deanship becomes a career capstone, the focus of your work and ministry needs to be your tenure in office. Whatever went on before you took office is not yours to own. When you leave, 90% of what you've done goes away, the next dean will do the work as she or he sees fit. When it's time to leave, just go, don't attempt to determine the outcome of the office or the school after your tenure, it's not your responsibility.

5. It's helpful to practice saying, "No." A wise and accomplished leader once told me, "Never underestimate the power of the baser motivations." While I don't spend much time questioning or interpreting people's motives, it is worth accepting that what motivates most people to ask something of the dean, from faculty to staff to students, has more to do with individual concerns and less to do with moving the organization forward. Deans need to remember that their position calls for being responsible for the welfare of the school as a whole, not for that of particular individuals. When a decision is needed, personal predilections, preferences, and peccadilloes need to take a back seat to the welfare of the school as a whole.

6. Make good friends with Edward Schein, Edwin Friedman, and Machiavelli. If you came into the dean's office from one of the classical academic disciplines it's likely you're not intimately familiar with this other trinity. If you want to

18

understand organizations, relationships, leadership and culture, those three will fill the gap in your education. The deanship calls for a re-education in matters of organizational leadership, institutional development, and understanding complex systems.

7. Choose a good President. He or she will help or hinder your work as dean. The same can be said about your registrar and administrative assistant--if you can find good ones, they're worth their weight in gold.

8. If you don't know about assessment or educational administration you'd better learn quickly. Educational leadership is planted in the field of higher education and deans are educational administrators. The work of the dean is increasingly a specialized function. Learn about rubrics, metrics, dashboards, project management, program level goals, learning outcomes, program development, market analysis, budgeting, as well as organizational and curriculum assessment. You'll do well, also, to learn the language of organizational bureaucracy, from state and federal DOE regs to accreditation standards.

9. The deanship is its own vocation and requires its own scholarship. While a dean may be a member of the faculty, his or her primary function is more centralized, administrative, supervisory, and managerial. In other words, a dean is not primarily a teaching faculty, functionally or pragmatically. The nature of the job just won't allow for it. The faculty member who takes on the role of dean will acquire a new profession with its particular skills, orientation, knowledge base, perspective, and discipline.

10. Network. Because the job of the dean is its own vocation and involves a high level of specialization, networking becomes an invaluable part of doing the job well. You can try to go it alone, but you and your school will benefit more when you seek out those relationships and resources that can help make you a better dean: connection with dean colleagues--experienced and novices, participation in professional organizations and gatherings of deans, etc. People are kind to sympathize about how busy, difficult, and challenging the work of the deanship is, but only other deans really understand. If you want to thrive as a dean, seek the support you need.

❖

Eight Challenges You WILL Face During Your Tenure as Dean

One of my favorite cartoons depicts a bowling pin on a psychiatrist's coach. There is a diploma on the wall, a plant in the corner, and a therapist with notepad sitting behind the disconcerted bowling pin character. The caption has the cartoon bowling pin asking, simply, "Why me?"

If you're a leader in the organization, it does little good to ask, "Why me?" when troubles and challenges come your way. If you're a leader, you're the 1-pin in the lineup for misplaced anxiety, complaints, and blame. Leaders are the point person for anxiety in any system. It just comes with the job. As second-chair leaders who lead from the center of the organization, challenges are to be expected in the job of the dean. For deans, asking "Why me?" is a meaningless question. The better question related to who must deal with problems and challenges in the school is, "Who else but me? I'm the dean!"

It may seem, given the average tenure of school deans (4.5 years), most would be able to avoid major crises and challenges. Alas, that is not the case. Here are eight challenges most deans can count on facing during their term in office.

Here are the eight challenges you *will* deal with as Dean:

1. Student Issues. At some point in your tenure you will likely need to be "the bad guy" and be the one who makes the call on dismissing a student. Whether for academic failures (plagiarism, cheating, a failing GPA), financial irresponsibility (a failure to pay tuition bills or housing rent, or accumulating debt over an established limit), a demonstrable lack of "fitness for ministry," or other offense or infraction, it is often the dean who is called upon to make the call. The issue of plagiarism alone is epidemic, and not likely to abate. Deans can count on having to deal with an increasing number of plagiarism cases in student academic work. While tragic and uncomfortable, it's worth accepting that, in some cases, dismissing a student is often the best thing to do, not only for the school, but for the student.

2. Faculty discontent. If you're doing the job right, you'll not be able to make everyone happy. Especially during times of institutional challenges, crises, or reorganization, during which difficult decisions need to be made, every decision will make someone upset--whether the decision affects them directly or not, and regardless that it was the right decision.

3. Presidential challenges. The relationship between a dean and the president is a critical one. It sets tone, helps or hinders making the vision a reality, and can help or hinder both the effectiveness of the organization and the cultural working environment. Leading from the middle, deans often are caught in triangles with the president on one corner, the dean on the other, and fill-in-the-blank on the third (faculty members, students, trustees, donors, and any number of issues, like interpretations about the vision, ideas about priorities, and expectations).

Additionally, most deans can count on a presidential transition-- an entering president, an exiting president, a presidential transitioning process. Some deans may need to deal with a president who defects in place, resulting in a leadership vacuum. Others may find themselves having to coach and educate a new president about the odd world of school culture for those who come in from outside the field of education (e.g., an accomplished leader in the world of business).

4. Financial challenges. Whether a school is endowment rich or tuition-challenged, most deans will experience financial challenges of some kind during their tenure. At worst, a dean will be called upon to help navigate the institution during a time of declared financial exigency. Less toxic challenges may include pushing for raises during belt-tightening, making a case for new scholarships, dealing with the distribution of resources in the face of the limitation of means, or making do with creative technological patchwork for instructional technologies that are quickly becoming obsolete and ineffective.

5. Staff changes and conflicts. Most people in an organization tend to work under the illusion of a sense of permanence and stability. From their vantage points, however, deans see the constant nature of change in the organization, including people entering and leaving. Workforce turnover brings with it the constant need for orientation, training, and adaptation to new relationships and work functions in the culture of the school. In addition, deans can count on having to deal with staff and employee conflict of some sort any given year. It is not uncommon for a dean to be involved in the dismissal process of a staff member during her or his tenure. Deans will be wise to anticipate this likelihood and to be proactive in establishing practices and procedures for handling the firing of personnel (hint: maintain detailed documentation!).

6. Curricular challenges. Course schedules and budgets are perpetual moving targets, both of which can contribute to curricular challenges. Whether dealing with curriculum assessment, a dreaded curriculum revision, or creating or closing a degree program, deans can count on facing challenges related to curricula almost daily. Curricula have a short shelf life, four to five years. It's not unusual for some schools to maintain a curriculum program for 10 years with a little tweaking here and there. Ultimately, those tweaks start to cause the program of study to implode due to the unsystematic band-aid approach to addressing programmatic challenges, student profile changes, and faculty changes. One of the biggest curricular challenges, of course, will be faced by deans whose tenure in office coincides with an accreditation visit.

7. Legal challenges. As unlikely as it may seem, it's not unusual for a dean to face legal issues during his or her tenure. These can range from a nuisance (a subpoena for student records, a call from an office in the DOE, or a consultation with the school's lawyer on a policy or governance issue) to being named in a lawsuit against the school. It's unlikely this likelihood is even mentioned in the job description you were presented with when interviewing for the job. When legal challenges present themselves as part of the dean's job, your school's attorney becomes your best friend.

8. Personal Challenges. Given a dean can face any or all of the above challenges, it's no surprise that other challenges will be of a more personal nature. Few can appreciate the pressures and work load of the deanship. Deans will likely face personal challenges of all sorts, though not all will be toxic or detrimental to their well-being. There will be personal challenges related to competency and self-doubt, to character and personal integrity, relationships and loneliness, personal goals and stamina, and vocation and meaning, just to mention a few.

If you're a dean, you WILL deal with more than one of these issues during your tenure (and some hapless deans will face them all!), and it will make little sense to ask, "Why me?" No academic institution can afford to have its leaders defect in place merely because a situation is uncomfortable. While this may not be welcomed news, to be forewarned is to be forearmed, as they say. When these challenges come up we may be tempted to cry, "They didn't train me to deal with these things!" The uncomfortable truth is there's little by way of training that prepares one to deal with complex crises. These challenges come with the job. How many have you experienced so far?

❖

Four Blind Spots Every Dean Needs to Avoid

One of the biggest liabilities for leaders in any system, including deans, is blind spots. Blind spots can be the result of personal bias, or of having inaccurate or insufficient information. When leaders fail to have a systemic perspective, 360-degree vision, or a "view from the balcony," all sorts of liabilities and handicaps result. A dean who is not aware of her or his blind spots may experience things a lot messier than they really are, or, perceive things are humming along more smoothly than is actually the case. Unaware of systemic dynamics, deans may tend to blame themselves for things that are not their fault, or, blame unfairly others for things not of their doing. Lacking clear-eyed vision, deans may misinterpret experiences and events they need to address. In any case, blind spots can result in what any leader least desires: SURPRISES!

Here are four blind spots every dean needs to avoid:

1. Spatial Blind Spots. A dean who suffers from spatial blind spots fails to see the school system as a whole. This is a liability that can be the result of the myopia of the daily administrivia that makes up most of the work week for the academic dean. As persons who lead from the middle, deans need to understand how all parts of the system influence each other---and, the persons in it. Here are signs that you may be experiencing spatial blindness:

- Focusing on what is happening to you but failing to see what is happening elsewhere in the system
- Failing to see what others are experiencing and dealing with in other parts of the system
- Failing to see how academic and curricular decisions (or non-decisions) impacts others in the system
- Failing to see how others' experience impacts your role in the system
- Thinking of persons in terms of stereotypes in the system ("Faculty always . . . ," "Staff are just . . . ," "Trustees never. . . .")
- Taking personally things that are not personal (just because it involves you as the dean, it doesn't mean it's *about* you).

2. Temporal Blind Spots. Temporal blind spots refers to our failure to interpret our context in the arch of its history. We all come into a system at one point in its history. That history provides a narrative arch that informs identity, has shaped a culture, created patterns and habits, and cultivated corporate values over time. It is the explanation to "We've never done it what way before" and the answer to the question "Why do we do it this way?" There are liabilities when deans do not avoid temporal blindness. We may tend to:

- Analyze only the present situation but fail to understand how the past influences current challenges
- Experience the stress of the moment but fail to account for the forces that led to the experience
- Fail to appreciate the history that brought about the present
- Misdiagnose the situation due to a lack of contextual and historical perspective
- Try to fix what doesn't need fixing (and fail to fix what does need fixing).

3. Relational Blind Spots. Relational blind spots refers to a failure to see how the structure, processes, and culture of the system impacts the experience of persons in it. Some liabilities of relational blindness are:

- Failing to see the ways in which the dean exists in systemic relationships with others
- Failing to see our functional position in the system, as opposed to merely the role we play when carrying the title "dean"
- Experiencing personal stress and pain by personalizing relational issues that belong to the system, or to others in the system
- Failing to appreciate the need to "stay connected" to others in the system beyond those most immediately in the "academic" and "administrative" spheres.

4. Process Blind Spots. Process blind spots refers to the failure to see and understand the organic dynamics that influence the system. Every organization and system comprises a "field," and the dynamics within that field has more influence than we tend to appreciate. Some liabilities deans may face from process blindness can be:

- A failure to differentiate procedure from process
- A failure to see the underlying dynamics that are influencing the way people are functioning
- A failure to take into account dynamics that can block or sabotage initiatives, vision, or plans (homeostasis, reactivity, etc.)
- Failing to address the correct level of change required (structural vs. cultural, administrative vs. programmatic, etc.)
- A failure to understand how the dynamics at work in the field is influencing the dean's own perception and thinking
- Failing to see the system as an integrated whole, as part of an emotional field, and over-compartmentalizing when addressing challenges and problems.

Which of the four blind spots do you think you are most prone to develop?

Do you have practices in place that help you check for your blind spots?

Are you aware of your personal biases in the four areas which lead to potential blind spots: spatial, temporal, relational, and process?

Which blind spot has been your greatest liability?

Adapted from Berry Oshry, *Seeing Systems: Unlocking the Mysteries of Organizational Life* (San Francisco: Berrett-Koehler Publishers, 2007).

❖

Paradoxes of Educational Leadership

At a gathering of school deans one activity had the deans share the job descriptions from each of their schools. This group of deans was from a variety of contexts: different geographic regions, trade and liberal arts schools, junior colleges and universities, free-standing and university-embedded schools, and from large and small institutions. After comparing their documents and position descriptions the insight emerged: everyone had pretty much the same job description. As the conversation continued, however, it became clear that while everyone in the room had the same job, they each served varied functions in their institutions.

The important insight gained from the activity is there's a difference between role and function. Every dean plays the same role (hence, all job descriptions look similar). Context, however, determines the function the dean actually serves in the organization. Ultimately, it became clear to the deans that the question is not "What does a dean do?" (they all did pretty much the same thing), rather, the real question is, "Given the context of the school, what is a dean to do?" The answer to that question is a product of the situated context in which a school resides.

The Paradox of the Deanship

The differentiation of role from function highlights one of the paradoxes of a vocation full of paradoxes. Regardless of what the job description says, the dean's effectiveness lies more in fulfilling the necessary *functions* of the office than in the prescribed role of the job. Leadership is more a function of the system than of personal characteristics or an individual's traits. Function is determined by context, which includes a school's culture, its organizational structure and polity, the particular trajectory of its organizational development, and the institutional lifespan stage during which the dean serves. The function of the dean will also be framed by the function of the office of the school's president, which also must differentiate between role and function.

Six Leadership Paradoxes

A common paradox is the often prickly relationship between a school's Faculty and its dean. Setting aside the common remarks of "having gone to the dark side" when a faculty member becomes dean, there are real tensions that arise between a dean that must be a steward of the institution and a Faculty that is grounded in the important work of teaching and scholarship.

- Faculty desire a powerful dean who can solve the school's problems, yet they are inherently suspicious of strong leadership.
- Faculty desire a dean who is a colleague-scholar but is an administrative pragmatist.

- Faculty desire a compassionate dean, yet need a leader who can be cunning and ruthless when necessary.
- Faculty want a dean who is fair, but desire preferential accommodation to personal needs and wants.
- Faculty want a powerful, self-confident dean, yet are suspicious of one who appears politically astute.
- Faculty expect their deans to be both pragmatic and visionary; to maintain the comfort of the status quo while moving the institutions in innovation, progress, and change.

Edwin Friedman, in *A Failure of Nerve: Leadership in the Age of the Quick Fix* stated, "The functioning of individuals in any institution is not determined by their nature (personality) but by their position within a relationship system, as well as by what other "cells" will permit them to do." Given these paradoxes, what is a dean to do, indeed?!

Five Operational Paradoxes

In addition to the leadership paradoxes, deans must also navigate operational paradoxes. For example, taking a cue from Charles Edmonson's *The Paradox of Leadership* here are some faced by deans:

1. A dean must be able to delegate responsibility while maintaining control. That's relatively easy when dealing with staff, but a challenge when it involves faculty members who function as "free agents."

2. A dean must be relentless while open-minded. To make progress the dean must maintain persistence of vision toward goals, but must be open to different strategies to get there.
3. A dean must conform to the culture in order to change it. This paradox is especially challenging for deans who come from outside the school's culture and system. A dean new to the system may need to take up to three years to understand the school's culture before substantive changes can be addressed.
4. A dean must practice pragmatic realism while maintaining optimism in the face of challenges and resistance. People in the system need a good dose of the reality of challenges and threats to the institution, but they also need hope.
5. A dean needs to promote institutional ideals without being idealistic. Ideals are important to the life of an institution, but ideals are abstract, ephemeral, and rarely realized. Hope, however, can provide the compass that gives an institution direction.
6. A dean understands that institutional adaptation often comes through crises and failures. Anxious organizations want guarantees and assurances from their leaders. Faculties, as a rule, are risk-averse. Yet risk is part of moving an organization forward, and risk can result in failure. However, learning from crises and failures are a part of how organizations move toward success.
7. Deans have authority without power. No matter how high up on the organizational chart the dean's office resides, it's a position with little actual power. Influence is how deans

get the job done, and influence is mediated by the quality of the relationships deans are able to cultivate.
8. A dean must ensure institutional compliance with external constraints (public expectations, accreditation standards, etc.) while striving to move from managerial maintenance to adaptive changes necessary for relevance, viability, if not survival.

The Ultimate Paradox

Perhaps the ultimate paradox of being a dean is that you are most effective in both role and function when nobody notices how good you are at the job. As Michael Shinagel, former dean of continuing education and University extension at Harvard University said, "The magic of leadership was best captured by Lao Tzu: "A leader is best when people barely know he exists, when his work is done, his aim fulfilled, they will say: we did it ourselves." This is the art of leadership at its best: the art that conceals art."

❖

Four Freaking Awesome Things About Being Dean

There are any number of reasons persons become school deans. Some reasons are personal, while some are a product of a particular context and its circumstance. In my experience, most deans answer the vocational calling of dean for good-intentioned reasons, sometimes, even noble ones. Most simply want to serve their institutions, despite the trade offs; they have gifts in administration, expertise in educational processes, perhaps even competencies in leadership. They are willing to make these capacities available to their organization, and when well-received, they are gifts to the institution. For a few, the deanship may become a permanent vocational calling. For others, the call to deanship will be for a short season. Even those who reluctantly accept the office will discover there are particular aspects of the work that, while challenging and at times overwhelming, can bring great satisfaction.

Deans may discover there are perks that come with the job they may not have anticipated. For example, here are five freaking awesome things about being a dean:

- You get to wear a cape to Faculty meetings if you want to
- You get first dibs on the school's timeshare in Boca Raton
- You gain immediate deference from faculty colleagues and unexpected instant respect from your estranged teenage children (and, your mother will be proud)
- You get a dean's slush fund.

Well, if you were enticed to take office with such promises, by now you've likely discovered that the job is little like what you imagined. However, there are some pretty awesome things about being an academic dean.

1. You get to work with some pretty smart people and passionate colleagues (although those two may not be the same persons).

Sometimes, when people ask me about what it's like to work in academia, I say, "It's not the real world, but I like it." It's a rare privilege to be in a context that provides the luxury of being around people who are paid to think deep thoughts, work with big ideas, and engage mind and spirit in the pursuit of ideals and noble work. Given the challenges faced by schools we can wonder how long that privileged professorial life can be sustained. But in the meantime, being around the rarefied air of scholars can be one of the most enriching parts of being a dean.

2. You get to shape the life of an institution.

Relatively few people get to be in a position to practice generativity at an institutional level to the capacity that is available to Presidents and Deans. It is a high calling to provide meaningful stewardship to a vision and institutionalized values that spans generations. As second chair leaders, deans, perhaps more that presidents, have the opportunity to interpret and shape the vision of the institution. While academic deans will tend to be behind-the-scene persons, their influence on the institution is immeasurable---one we all hope, is for the good.

3. You can make a difference in times of challenge and crises.

The historical narrative of every institution includes nodal periods of crises where survival was in the balance. In every instance the key to moving from survival to thriving was the presence of committed and capable leaders who had the grit to hang on and move forward when others would quit. Everyone admires successful individuals and institutions, but they both had one thing in common most don't consider: they never quit when the going got rough. When it would seem that shutting down the enterprise or just walking away was easier, they personalized the vision, rolled up their sleeves, and did whatever it took to find the way.

For better or ill, and despite wishing it to be otherwise, a dean's greatest opportunities to bring about change and make a difference come during predictable and unpredictable nodal events involving crisis. These provide time and opportunity to "open up the system" and disrupt the normalcy of homeostasis. These nodal events can be a curriculum revision, a troubling accreditation report, faculty hires or dismissals, governance crises (e.g., Presidential transitions, a merger); institutional crises (e.g., financial duress, campus downsizing or relocations). Every dean can anticipate having to deal with at least one major crisis during her or his tenure. For deans who want to make a difference, the mantra is, "Never waste a crisis!"

Deans today serve during a time of unprecedented change and challenge for higher education. One question of perspective is, twenty-five years from now, after this liminal epoch for higher education, what will be said of the deans who led their institutions during this time?

4. You will acquire the capacity for leadership.

A perpetual dilemma for schools is how to help students become leaders through an academic curriculum. Most schools make good effort by providing practical opportunities in various contexts. But that is of limited effect. The reality is that one can only learn leadership when one is in a position that carries the responsibility and burden of leadership, and requires one to function as leader in a context that recognizes one as the *de facto* leader in the system. Faculty members may refer to themselves "a leader in my field," but that metaphor does not come close to the realities of being a leader in a system. Should a person move from faculty member to dean in her or his context, that insight comes pretty quickly.

Being a leader requires a change of perspective, stance, functioning, priorities, the burden of responsibilities, and the cultivation of courage one did not need before---even in one's same context. Shifting to a position of leader will expand your understanding and perspective of a school, and, of its mission. It is likely those would remain out of your reach until accepting the call to be dean. And for certain, you'll never talk about leadership to students the same way as you may have before.

❖

Fixing the Problems of Higher Education

My engineer son has a mantra: *"Fix the problem."* As mantras go, it's a pretty good one. Simple, memorable, intuitive, and to the point. The mantra refers to our tendency to go about addressing issues and problems by doing a lot of things, but none of which will actually *fix the problem.* In short, it is a reminder to focus on the cause and not the symptom, which is a persistent and common tendency.

Simply by virtue of the nature of the job, school deans need to be problem solvers. The unprecedented challenges of today's pressures on schools--financial, cultural, institutional, educational, and professional--makes this singular capacity arguably one of the important for today's deans. It is likely that in colleges and universities no other person is in the position to be able to address the multiple problems facing the school than the one who leads from the center and is connected to every strand in the complex web of the system.

Recently, in the faculty and staff lounge of a school someone had the ability to "solve the problem." The problem was with the coffee pot. Despite years of reminder memos, signs, and complaints, inevitable the "last person" to use the coffee pot or leave the lounge at the end of the day would not turn off the unit. (First logical problem: how do you know you're the "last person" to leave a room?). This resulted in the roasting of the dregs in the glass coffee pot with its attending burnt-coffee smell and potential fire hazard.

One staff member finally fixed the problem. Rather than try to change people's behavior by attempting to make them more responsible, posting another memo, sending another pleading email to the entire distribution list, or putting up another sign, he got a wall outlet timer, set it to shut off automatically at the end of the day, and plugged in the coffee pot. Problem solved.

It's An Age-old Situation

I recently came across this way of making the point for the need to "fix the problem" (and not something else). You may have seen it:

The Tribal wisdom of the North American Indian, passed on from generation to generation, says that, "When you discover that you are riding a dead horse, the best strategy is to dismount."

However, in the world of higher education more advanced strategies are often employed, such as:

- Buying a stronger whip.
- Changing riders.
- Appointing a faculty committee to study the horse.
- Arranging to visit other institutions to see how they ride horses.
- Lowering the standards so that dead horses can be included.
- Reclassifying the dead horse as living-impaired.
- Outsourcing the issue of dead horses overseas.
- Hiring outside consultants to ride the dead horse.
- Harnessing several dead horses together to increase speed.
- Providing additional funding and/or training to increase dead horse's performance.
- Hiring an educational consultant to teach faculty and administrators to ride a dead horse more efficiently
- Conducting a survey to see if lighter riders would improve the dead horse's performance.

- Declaring that as the dead horse does not have to be fed, it is less costly, carries lower overhead and therefore contributes substantially more to the bottom line of the mission and budget than do some other horses.
- Rewriting the expected performance requirements for all horses.
- Promoting the dead horse to a supervisory position.

A Broken Educational Industry?

Many will argue the problem is that the traditional ways of education are broken----extended years of required study in residence, ineffective pedagogies, and an over focus on scholarship at the expense of practical wisdom. Others argue the problem is an ivory tower disconnect with the real-world challenges of the world today, and for others, the problems are an unsustainable business model and declining support from all sectors. For others, the problem is simply a declining perceived relevance and worth of a graduate degree.

In addition to the perceptions of the problem, there are factual evidences of the challenges schools face including, a changing faculty profile, the failure in cultivating minority leadership, shrinking financial resources, declining enrollments, rising student debt, changing student profiles, accreditation challenges related to changes in higher education, and crushing campus and facilities overhead for a possibly obsolete educational system. That what extent these challenges are actually problems may be open to debate. To some extent a dean may approach these as challenges or problems depending on whether she or he is a glass-half-full or half-empty kind of person.

Obstacles to Solving the Problem

As critical as is the function of solving problems to the role of the dean, there are obstacles to the attempt itself. Any dean attempting to bring about innovative and imaginative solutions to problems is rarely met with enthusiastic affirmation. In fact, if anything, denial and sabotage are the common first response from any system challenged think and act different---regardless of how creatively practical the solution and how dire the problem. Meaning, solving complex institutional problems is inherently difficult in ways that have nothing to do with the problems themselves.

Yet another challenge is the matter of the obstacles to creative problem-solving deans themselves face. David A. Owens, in *Creative People Must Be Stopped,* identified six ways innovation is killed in organizations. Any dean attempting to bring about innovative solutions to the challenging problems in her or his context will do well to be aware of these innovation killers. They are:

- Individual Constraints (personnel and personalities)
- Industry Constraints (accreditation agencies, Board of Education guidelines)
- Organizational Constraints (old structures, competing silos, cumbersome policies)
- Societal Constraints (loss of prestige, changing student demographics, shrinking support)
- Group Culture Constraints (academic guilds, homeostasis, turf wars, Faculty ethos, work environment)
- Technological Constraints (lack of technical expertise or resources).

In complex systems, such as a colleges and universities, deans attempting to address the deeper problems will tend to face multiple constraints that resist their solution. In attempting to solve the problems of the school, it will help to (1) identify the *problem*, and (2) accurately assess the constraints that will inhibit finding the solution. In addition, the most effective deans will persistently ask to what extent they themselves are a constraint to progress and change.

❖

Physics for Deans

An academic dean friend of mine once asked in frustration, "Why is this work so hard?!" I'm not sure I know the answer to that question. Some jobs are just more challenging due to the complexity of the work and the span of responsibility. But, here are eleven inviolable scientific laws that (playfully and unscientifically) may help explain why the job of the academic dean is so hard (or, why it's almost impossible to get things done).

1. Heisenberg's Uncertainty Principle

This principle states that two complementary parameters (such as position and momentum, energy and time) cannot both be known to infinite accuracy; the more you know about one, the less you know about the other. The same tends to be true in an organization. You'll never know everything that goes on in the institution. The more you focus on one thing (e.g, assessment, personnel issues, re-writing the academic manuals), the less you'll be able to give attention to other things. Corollary: Intuition is necessary for academic leadership. Sometimes, you just have to feel your way through a situation because you'll never know everything you need. *Rule*: Sometimes, when you need to make a decision, the data will not help, just go with your gut.

2. The Complementarity Principle

The principle that a given system cannot exhibit both wave-like behavior and particle-like behavior at the same time. That is, certain experiments will reveal the wave-like nature of a system, and certain experiments will reveal the particle-like nature of a system, but no experiment will reveal both simultaneously. Corollary: How people view you as dean will be complimentary to their place in the system, and based on their perspective of reality. You'll be viewed by some as a good dean and by others as a poor one, but not both simultaneously. *Rule*: While people's perspective may define their reality, and their relationship with you as dean, at the end of the day, it's your own perspective that counts. Set your own standards.

3. Archimedes' Principle:

A body that is submerged in a fluid is buoyed up by a force equal in magnitude to the weight of the fluid that is displaced, and directed upward along a line through the center of gravity of the displaced fluid. Corollary: When you submerge yourself in (the fluid of) your context you will displace things toward the center of gravity you set for your organization. *Rule*: Strive to displace the bad stuff in your system and let the good stuff float to the top. The *gravitas* of the dean's office can provide a deep center of gravity.

4. Brownian Motion

The continuous random motion of solid microscopic particles when suspended in a fluid medium due to the consequence of ongoing bombardment by atoms and molecules. Corollary: Organizations need someone in the system to provide direction. Work to align the particles in your system to move toward the same direction with intention and purpose. Random activities will get you nowhere. *Rule*: Learn the art of politics: the ability to get people to join together for the common good.

5. Coriolis Pseudoforce

A pseudoforce which arises because of motion relative to a frame of reference which is itself rotating relative to a second, inertial frame. The magnitude of the Coriolis "force" is dependent on the speed of the object relative to the noninertial frame, and the direction of the "force" is orthogonal to the object's velocity. Corollary: A school does not exist in a vacuum. It is subject to the forces and influences in the "fields" of higher education, the matrix of competing schools and programs, economic forces, etc. How fast you can make progress in your school is often determined by larger issues outside your control. Additionally, the speed of progress you can achieve in one area is often dependent on the relative speed of change in another area in the institution. *Rule*: Be judicious about what things you need to speed up and what things can wait.

6. Dalton's Law of partial pressures

The total pressure of a mixture of ideal gases is equal to the sum of the partial pressures of its components; that is, the sum of the pressures that each component would exert if it were present alone and occupied the same volume as the mixture. Corollary: deans need to introduce a certain amount of pressure and anxiety into the system to bring about change and progress. However, systems can only tolerate a certain amount of pressure. Too little and there is not sufficient motivating force for change; too much and the system gives in to despair and frustration. Deans are often the safety valve in the system who regulate for optimum pressure. *Rule*: Discomfort is a motivator for change; satisfaction is not. Maintain the appropriate level of discomfort in your system.

7. Equivalence Principle

The basic postulate of Einstein's general theory of relativity, which posits that an acceleration is fundamentally indistinguishable from a gravitational field. Corollary: Often, it seems we are not making progress at any give moment. Sometimes it seems the amount of progress deans are able to make is in direct inverse proportion to the amount of effort they exert. It takes persistence of vision to get to the point where momentum breaks into escape velocity. Getting past institutional inertia means working through the drag of homeostasis and resistance in the system. *Rule*: It's always too soon to quit; in organizations, progress happens slow and steady

8. Hooke's Law

The stress applied to any solid is proportional to the strain it produces within the elastic limit for that solid. The constant of that proportionality is the Young modulus of elasticity for that substance. Corollary: similar to Dalton's Law, strain, crises, and challenge help cultivate adaptation in the system. Effective deans never waste a crisis. They allow pain to be a motivator for change. How much stress can you put on your system when trying to bring about change? What is the capacity for adaptation in your system? Rule: Institutions can bear more stress than we assume. Remember that threat yields adaptation, while resilience is a product of catastrophe. It's easier to work on adaptive change than to deal with the experience of resilience.

9. Newton's Law of universal gravitation

Two bodies attract each other with equal and opposite forces; the magnitude of this force is proportional to the product of the two masses and is also proportional to the inverse square of the distance between the centers of mass of the two bodies. Corollary: Health attracts health and dysfunction attracts dysfunction. This may answer the question of why anyone would want the job of dean, and, why the school picked YOU. Healthy and adaptive systems are able to attract leaders who will challenge the organization toward development, growth, and into the changes necessary. Immature and anxious systems seek leaders who will ease their anxiety and solve their problems for them. In other words, dysfunctional systems want a superhero or a wizard, not a leader. What is your system asking of you? *Rule*: Challenge promotes growth; coddling promotes dependence.

10. van der Waals force

Forces responsible for the non-ideal behavior of gases, and for the lattice energy of molecular crystals. There are three causes: dipole-dipole interaction; dipole-induced dipole moments; and dispersion forces arising because of small instantaneous dipoles in atoms.* Corollary: deans need to be the "positive deviant" in the system, the one who can bring positivity to the system in the form of respectful relationships, transparent communication, and trust in the midst of disagreement. Leadership is not about power, despite the common application of that concept to leadership. Strictly speaking, power is energy divided by time. Those who make leadership an issue of power merely invite conflict and resistance. Leadership, however, is about influence, and that is mediated by the nature of the relationships you are able to cultivate with those in your system. *Rule*: Deans lead through influence.

11. Murphy's Law

If anything can go wrong, it will. Corollary: None needed. *Rule*: "Stuff" happens.

❖

Leadership Secrets of Effective Deans

I find a lot of natural connection between the functioning of effective school deans and August Turak's list of "11 Leadership Secrets You've Never Heard About"

Credit given for a catchy title, but these are more proven common-sense realities than "secrets." Most experienced and effective leaders know these, and, effective deans need to know these too. So, with apologies to Mr. Turak, here's a spin on academic leadership secrets you MAY not have heard about.

1. Effective Deans seize the initiative. Or, as we deans like to say, "Never waste a crisis." Sometimes you have to wait for the right timing to make a change, other times you need to create the opportunity and conditions for change. Either way, more often than not, the only place initiative happens will be from the office of the dean. Practice initiative.

2. Effective Deans create their own jobs. All academic deans have the same job (and all job descriptions read similar), but, context determines function. What does your school need of its dean, and why are YOU the dean and not another? An old adage in education is, "A school reflects its leader." Cast your own shadow and throw it long.

3. Effective Deans are coachable. There's a steep learning curve for new deans. You'll be more effective and keep your sanity if you cultivate a new network of coaches, mentors, and experts. Join a dean's listserve, attend professional, , join educational administration networks. When you need help, ask for it, and, when you create something useful in your work, share your stuff.

4. Effective Deans anticipate. As second chair leaders deans need to take the long view. Plan your curriculum schedule five years out (no, really); sketch a six year faculty development plan (retirements, hires, sabbaticals, etc.); anticipate presidential transitions; plan for your own development in office, or, for succession. Given the nature of the job and how organizations and human nature deal with change, anticipate that every new initiative, vision, or novel idea, however appropriate, will be met with resistance.

5. Effective Deans are great communicators. This includes communicating the good and the bad, and, always telling the truth. Learn to create infographics! During times of crisis and high anxiety, you can never over-communicate.

6. Effective Deans are goal driven. Educational institutions cannot afford a "maintenance" mentality. Deans need to initiate action and push against inertia. Presidents maintain the institutional vision; Deans work to realize the goals.

7. Effective Deans show, don't tell. Demonstrate the values and ethos you want to cultivate in your school's culture: professionalism, consideration, excellence, dependability, accountability, trustworthiness, grace, etc. One burden of leadership is, you have to set the standards, and then keep them.

8. Effective Deans earn trust. Just as importantly, Deans will need to maintain trust. At points along the way you'll need to make difficult decisions that affect people at some level. As appropriate as your decision will be, some will feel betrayed. Consistently acting with integrity and telling the truth will help maintain trust, even when people choose to be mistrustful.

9. Effective Deans offer solutions. A major part of a dean's job is to solve problems--institutional, and sometimes, other people's problems. See last month's post on problem solving for more. Effective deans know to never bring a problem to the President without also bringing a solution.

10. Effective Deans are sympathetic. But remember that your primary responsibility is the welfare of the school. You can be sympathetic and still say "No," to personal requests or demands of privilege that do not serve the school as a whole.

11. Effective Deans are loyal. As leaders from the center, deans need to be able to send the message, "I have your back," to both President and Faculty. That's a tough one to pull off. This only happens when you are first loyal to your own calling, your own principles and values, and your own commitment to the calling of your office.

❖

Nine Ways to Dean Like a Pirate

I have a couple of friends who are really into "Talk Like a Pirate Day"(September 19 in case you're wondering). One of them dresses up like a pirate for the day (in Johnny Depp "Pirates of the Caribbean" style) and plays the part to the hilt, sometimes visiting local elementary schools to the delight, and confusion, of children. I think there may be some things school deans can learn from pirates. While pillaging and looting to help offset the academic administrative budget may not be recommended, here are nine ways you can dean like a pirate:

1. Look the part and act the part. Many deans suffer from the "Impostor Syndrome" when they first take the job. Some humbler souls have difficulty being "first among equals" with faculty colleagues. Some feel uneasy with the deference given to them that comes with the office. It is worth remembering, however, that deans are academic leaders, and leadership has more to do with what the system needs of its leader and less about any insecurities one may have about playing the role. And, it can't hurt to literally dress the part of the office, which can call for gravitas and decorum. One faculty member was overheard saying of his dean, "I never can tell if he's working or going to the gym."

2. Treat Faculty as Maties, but don't forget you're the First Mate. Faculty members are smart, some are experts in their field, but they tend not the be "smart" about the larger picture of the institution: how the organization works, the minutia of accreditation issues, the critical roles played by non-teaching and support staff, or the interrelated, the necessary expedience of political relationships, and the interconnected nature of the curriculum and its impact on everything from student recruitment and retention to the economics of the institution. On occasion, a faculty member will forget they are also employees of the institution, believing themselves to be "free agents." One dean noted of his Faculty, "Individually, they're some of the smartest people around, but in times of high anxiety, their collective IQ can drop 20 points." Treat Faculty with respect, strive to remove obstacles to their work of scholarship and teaching, but accept the liability that comes with needing to be liked above being an effective educational leader. Remember what author Henry Cloud says to leaders, "You are ridiculously in charge."

3. Prepare for turbulent waters and storms. Schools are institutions that are sensitive to shifts in the larger environment. Smaller liberal arts colleges, for example, have been called the canaries in the mine shaft of higher education. For deans, the job can sometimes feel like going from one small crisis to another, but you can also count on facing at least one major storm during your tenure--institutional financial distress, employee or faculty dismissals, faculty revolts, lawsuits, accreditation notations, conflicts with the President and/or Board members, all loom just over the horizon. Anticipate the storms. You'll not only need to manage yourself, but also provide leadership for others in the system to weather the storm.

4. Keep things shipshape. Quality control, accreditation compliance, and maintaining institutional, programmatic and personal integrity all fall within the dean's charge. Effective educational leaders know that everything matters--"small details" are ignored at your peril. Every accommodation to a plea for exemption from policy has an unintended consequence. Keeping things shipshape is not sexy, and no one will thank you for it. But when its neglect starts causing problems, you'll be the one at whom people point fingers, and rightly so.

5. Keep the wind in your institutional sails. Every once in a while, get up on the crow's nest and look out over the horizon to gain perspective. Suck in a lungful of sea air to clear your mind and let the vista inspire you. Invest in your own professional development as dean, and insist on a faculty culture and ethos that values professional development of your teaching faculty and of your staff. At the end of the decade the educational institutions that will be thriving will be the ones who have been imaginative enough to change, fleet enough to do so, and who have had the visionary leaders to get them there.

6. Seek a safe harbor during attacks and times of stress. During your tenure as dean you can count on at least one instance of being under attack. Get a coach or support system to help you manage stress and anxiety. Stay close to your president, who should be an ally. Remember that 90% of the problems you'll face will not about you personally, they just come with the job. Maintain a real life, cultivate your spirituality, practice grace.

7. The Plank. Deans need to guard against toxic attitudes and behaviors from staff and Faculty for the welfare of the school. It is likely that during your tenure you'll need to address personnel issues that call for dismissal of underfunctioning, underperforming, misfit, insubordinate, or acting out staff or faculty members. When things get to the point where a parting of ways becomes the right thing to do, deans need to accept it's appropriate to help someone walk the plank.

8. Check your compass often. In the midst of the daily barrage of administrivia to which deans must give attention, it's important to check your compass to make sure you're headed in the right direction. Will all your activities, plans, and meetings help move you toward your institutional goals? Does your curriculum help your students move in the right vocational direction? Do your metrics provide the correct waypoints to get you where you are going? Is your institution headed in the right direction?

9. Create your treasure map. Working for mere survival is not enough, though that can seem to fill most days for an institution under duress. But people need something higher than keeping the boat afloat to get up in the morning. Everyone on board needs to have a sense of purpose. What is the ultimate goal worth pursuing for your school? Where does your treasure lie? Keeping the mission and vision of the school before your mates will help everyone row in the same direction.

❖

Five Essential Functions of the Dean

I agree with Stephen Graham's assertion that "Right now, . . . schools need leaders, not just managers."[1] Specifically addressing . . . school deans, he wrote that , ". . . schools need leaders who are willing to name the changes that have taken place, anticipate the changes to come, and lead their schools into the path that will enable them to be faithful to their heritages and stories and also to engage the new conditions that face them."[2]

I think that holds true for deans in any educational institution. What may not be clear in the wake of that perspective is that school deans need to be *educational* leaders. Meaning, the position they hold in a school, and the function of leadership called for, requires that they think and lead educationally as much as philosophically, academically, or scholarly. The key concept here is that leadership is always a function of the system, much less so a function of personality.

Effective leaders are those who provide the functions their systems need of them. The consistent counter-intuitive reality is that effective schools have strong leaders—conversely, it is not always the case that strong leaders have effective schools. The question every dean and administrator needs to ask then, is, "What function will I need to provide to be an effective dean?"

The literature of educational leadership has identified five essential functions of leaders in educational institutions. While the list has appeared in different forms over the years, basically, they are:

1. Having a vision and communicating it well
2. Articulating goals and identifying strategies
3. Creating an adaptive culture open to change
4. Monitoring progress
5. Providing necessary interventions.[3]

All educational leaders need to provide those essential functions, but, there's no one best way to provide them. WHAT a dean, as educational leader, needs to provide is clear; HOW a particular dean chooses to go about it is a product of both context and personality.

The challenge of the complex nature of the job, with its multi-faceted dimensions, calls for an astonishing wide-ranging skills set: from interpersonal relational skills to high-level analytical and intuitive-interpretive skills. Deans need to cultivate and apply a wide repertoire of cognitive styles in order to carry out the job, sometimes, in the course of a single day! They need often to switch from abstract, symbolic perspectives to a concrete, realistic perspective from one moment to the next. They may start the day with internal vision-casting in a Zen-like state while driving to the office, only to be engulfed in managerial problem-solving within twenty minutes of sitting at the desk, then, end the day dealing with interpersonal conflicts in the midst of emotional reactivity.

Effective deans do well to remember that in the midst of the urgency and the press of the daily triage, there are only five functions that will ultimately determine their effectiveness. Five things make the difference, for they are the essential functions that the school, as a system, needs of its academic leader. It is not much of an overstatement to say that, at the end of the day, all else is distraction. In fact, what dysfunctional systems are very good at is distracting its leader from focusing on and providing the essential functions!

- To what extent are you providing the five essential educational functions of a dean?
- What things distract you from investing time, thought, and effort on the five essential functions?
- Are you stronger in providing one function over others? Which functions do you need to work on increasing your competence?
- Dysfunctional systems are adept at sabotaging a leader's focus on the five functions. Are you able to identify ways your system and context inhibits your effectiveness in one or more of the five essential functions?

[1] *(C(H)AOS Theory: Reflections of Chief Academic Officers in Theological Schools.* Wm. B. Eerdmans, 2011, p. 71
[2] Ibid.
[3] See for example Rutherford, W. L. "School Principals as Effective Leaders," *Phi Delta Kappan* 67 (1985): 31-34.

❖

The Political Dean

During a webinar on the topic of leadership I offered a list of important skills related to the topic at hand. The list included something along the lines of the need for a leader to be "politically astute." That item, only one among several, got the most questions and comments during the Q&A segment, with several participants expressing discomfort with the idea. That's not surprising. How often do we hear people express, "I just don't like the politics involved," or, "I enjoy the job, I just don't like the politics."?

The reality is, for better or worse, politics comes with the job of the academic dean. This can be grating and uncomfortable to some, especially to those who move into that role from the more pastoral academic life of scholar and teacher, where politics is sometimes studied but need not be practiced.

The situation is not helped by the preponderance of negative attitudes toward politics. Groucho Marx has been quoted as saying, "Politics is the art of looking for trouble, finding it everywhere, diagnosing it incorrectly and applying the wrong remedies." Neither is the negative perception helped by books like political scientist and game theorist William H. Riker's *The Art of Political Manipulation,* in which he offers twelve historical vignettes of how people have manipulated their opponents in order to win political advantage. And some definitions like "Politics is about who gets what, when, how," by notable political scientist Harold Lasswell, can only reinforce our cynicism.

But, we just can't get around the fact that effective deans are politically astute. It will help, however, to acquire a more positive understanding of the function of being political in one's context. People are, by nature, political claimed Aristotle. In other words, we are creatures whose nature it is to live and work in a *polis*. Most can assert the claims that "there is no self apart from community," that humans were created to be social beings, that being human is primarily a social phenomenon, etc.

A more hopeful and positive understanding about the role of politics in the work of the dean is Bismark's famous quote, "Politics is the art of the possible, the attainable---the art of the next best." Harvard Business School Professor Linda Hill observes that organizations are inherently political entities, and she argues that a leader's success is determined by how well she or he manages the political dynamics associated with all aspects of organizational life.

As educational leaders deans must negotiate the complex network of relationships that make up the school, with its wide matrix of relationships (partner schools, constituents, accrediting bodies, denominational entities, etc.). A politically astute dean provides several important functions to the system. Here are four:

1. Identifies the Common Good.

A perpetual struggle for schools is to overcome the "silo" structures that isolate key personnel whose work and contributions are critical to the mission of the school. Entrenched structures that isolate faculty by fields and guilds, faculty from staff, trustees from faculty, etc., only serve to fragment the system. It is ironic that in terms of modeling "a learning community," schools may be among the poorest examples. One important function of the political dean is to keep before all segments of the school the common good each participates in and to which they contribute. Academics and scholarship tend to be contexts of solitary enterprises. The political dean needs to remind everyone of mutual commitments to the corporate body and the institution.

2. Builds Consensus.

Politics includes negotiating for consensus and cooperation between factions within the organization. In this regard the political dean will need to be a pragmatist when others may work out of ideological or philosophical orientations. Pragmatism welcomes compromise. At its heart, politics is the art of getting people to join together for the common good. In the context of the often siloed culture of an academic institution, and with diminishing institutional resources, this political function can rise to the level of a fine art.

3. Helps People Commit to Action.

The political dean understands that consensus is not equivalent to commitment, and it does not automatically translate to action. It is not enough to get people to agree on something through consensus. A system needs persons who will commit to action, invest time, energy, and talent (and in times of crises, blood, sweat, and tears). The political dean understands that people are motivated by different things. For example, rarely is extra pay a motivator for Faculty, but it will tend to be for staff members. The political dean never underestimates the power of the baser motivations.

4. Builds Generative Networks.

No enterprise can succeed without a strong network of partners, supporters, and constituents. And rarely can a leader be effective without staying connected to people inside and outside the organization. The political dean understands the important of building generative networks. A good strategy for success, author Linda Hill advises, is to think about the people you depend on to help get your job done: "And then you have to ask yourself, 'Have I built the right relationships with those people? Do they really trust me? Do we have mutual expectations? Can I influence them?

Can they influence me?" If the answers are no to those questions, says Hill, "then you have not built the right kind of relationships."

Hill also argues for networking outside the dean's immediate circle of peers and bosses, and building "mutual influence" with people outside the organization "over whom you don't have formal authority, but who in fact you need to do things for you in order for you to be successful, or for your team to be successful." In an age of scarcity the need to partner with like-minded organizations with similar or parallel missions becomes increasingly critical.

Networking seems to come naturally to extroverts, but can be a challenge to introverts. Managing and cultivating relationships often requires introverted deans to be social, even when they don't want to. Developing a "networking style" that fits who you are, is necessary, says Hill.

Resources for learning to be a political dean:

Cialdini, *Influence: The Psychology of Persuasion*. Harper Business, 2006.
Fisher and Ury, *Getting to Yes*. Penguin Books, 2011.
Hill and Lineback, *Being the Boss: The 3 Imperatives for Becoming a Great Leader*. Harvard Business Review Press, 2019.
Machiavelli, *The Prince*.
Ury, *Getting Past No: Negotiating in Difficult Situations*. Bantam, 1993.
Stone, et al., *Difficult Conversations: How to Discuss What Matters Most*. Penguin Books 2010.

❖

How Academic Institutions Stay Stuck

I've observed many academic leaders in the process of making decisions. Some pertain to organizational or institutional decisions (dealing with employees, closing a program, dealing with a crisis). In only a few of those instances have I observed persons making quick and decisive choices from several options and then moving toward a new direction. Most people struggle through a long winding, angst-filled process of uncertainty and indecision before achieving resolution and finding direction. Most seem unable to identify their options, much less come up with new ones.

As persons who "lead from the center," Deans in academic institutions need to help their organizations through change. That often involves helping the players make decisions: president, administration, faculty, program directors, sometimes even trustees. Given the particular culture of academic schools, which calls for some level of "shared governance" and the necessity to "bring people along," the potential for staying stuck may be a higher liability than in other contexts.

A major part of how organizations stay stuck has more to do with emotional process than with information and options. People can't get past the impasse of feelings that block their ability to make choices. But often people get stuck because they cannot think through an issue. We can identify three facets in the process of making a decision: the motivation facet, the thinking facet, and the decision facet. Each of those facets in the process requires the ability to think through the issues at hand. But each step holds the hazard of faulty thinking that keeps organizations stuck.

Here are examples of faulty thinking associated with each facet. Each can potentially keep a system stuck, and I've seen each of these operating in schools at one point or another:

The Motivation Facet

- Trying to reduce the discomfort of dissonance
- Seeking the comfort of internal alignment between the old and the new
- Being driven by feeling obliged to complete a public commitment or personal loyalties rather than working out of values, vision and principles
- Being driven by a desire for certainty or security
- Distorting memories or past decisions to make the current decisions seem good (regardless of how bad they actually may be)
- Soliciting confirmation that we are about to make a good decision (especially from people who have no stake in the outcome)
- Being driven by the Scarcity Principle: the fear of regret at not attaining something that is scarce
- Being immobilized by the Sunk-Cost Effect: being reluctant to pull out of an investment of money, energy, or effort even if it has yielded poor results.

The Thinking Facet

- Preferring a known probability to an unknown one
- Failing to compensate enough for our own bias
- Elaborating on likelihood: either thinking centrally or taking unthinking short-cut decisions
- Focusing on short-term benefits rather than long-term solutions
- Seeking more facts for making a decision, even when they are irrelevant
- Failing to critically assess source credibility: seeking input from people who we are likely to believe rather than those who have expertise.

The Deciding Facet

- Being stuck in the Augmentation Principle: the belief that evidence for a decision is accumulative
- Using only limited logic in making a decision
- Accepting simple, explainable hypotheses for complex situations and issues
- Failure to use the right strategies for different types of choice
- Deciding by comparing things falsely (apples to oranges).

Making a good decision is about choosing wisely from among options and choices. And while decision-making is both and emotional and an intellectual act, it's important to engage in "right thinking" in order to make right decisions. Because deans occupy a unique position in the system that provides a multi-faceted view of issues and challenges, they are vital to helping their schools get unstuck by avoiding the faulty thinking in each facet and step in decision-making. Finally, the best cure for being stuck is simply, to make a decision.

❖

The Dean in the Age of Change

During a meeting among deans they commiserated over how difficult it was to bring about changes in their schools. Despite their best efforts at communicating the urgent need for change, cultivating support, and implementing strategies, change was happening too slow or blocked by key players. In some cases, necessary changes were derailed as exasperated deans found it necessary, as one dean put it, "to pick my battles. I only have so much energy to give." As tends to be the case, bringing about change requires a constant push against inertia, at the very least. One dean commented that few in her system seemed able to see that "change is the constant." The people she most needed to help move the institution forward at times became the biggest obstacles to bringing about change.

A new kind of epoch

During the epochs of the "information age" and the "knowledge age," the role of the dean was relatively well-defined. Academic management and supervision were sufficient for the job. Deans who currently serve in educational institutions find themselves in an old role (a "medieval" role, as someone described it) in a new and different age. In an epoch of seismic change, the "transformation age," deans need to function as educational *leaders* who can not only maintain institutional integrity, but be the agents of change who will actually help transform their institutions.

According to Dale W. Lick, former university president and professor, "Transformation means a fundamental change in condition, nature, or function."[1] It is not longer a matter of doing the same things differently---it's a matter of doing different things.

Deans appreciate, if not always understand, the kinds of changes they must give attention to, and, the multiple levels those changes impact. Beyond programmatic changes, the fundamental changes that have seismic impact on their institutions include technological, communication, cultural, and economic. Each impacts on multiple levels, and include challenges to fundamental questions about mission, relationships, outcomes, the nature and value of education, identity, and institutional viability. The challenge is that a new epoch requires a new kind of dean.

A new kind of dean

In an epoch during which the speed, intensity, and magnitude of external changes are overwhelming many educational institutions, deans will need to redefine the role of chief academic officer. In the age of transformational change, deans need to expand their functions beyond managerial and programmatic competencies. One of the greatest needs of schools is that of the dean as academic leader, not merely administrator of educational programs or managers of institutional systems.

In their roles as institutional leaders, deans may serve four functions related to change in their institutions:

Dean as steward of change. The most traditional role of the dean in the institution is that of the steward of change. In this role a dean carries out the changes that are the initiatives from points of authority in the system: trustees, the office of the president, accrediting agencies, internal assessment or review groups, etc. This role consists of primarily administrative and supervisory functions. In some contexts the dean must also engage in evaluation, quality control, and compliance assurance activities. One aspect of this role is that the dean also becomes a target of change in that she or he must respond to the requirements placed on the office and its tasks.

Dean as advocate of change. In this role the dean is in the position of supporting institutional change but with no authority to make the necessary changes happen. The authority for the changes will reside in other agents (the board of trustees, departments, staff persons, the president, program leaders, committees, etc.). With no authority, the dean's advocacy will have impact to the extent he or she has influence in the system.

Dean as sponsor of change. In the role of sponsor of change a dean holds legitimate authority to advocate and lead institutional, programmatic, and personnel changes. Depending on the context and culture, the scope of this authority may be limited. In some contexts authority may not automatically include the influence necessary to help make changes happen. In other contexts, a lack of support from key influencers, or persons in authority, will limit the capacity of a dean to function as sponsor of change.

Dean as agent of transformative change. This is the new and emerging function of the academic leader, one who goes beyond management and supervision for maintaining existing systems, structures and cultures. Doing the same old thing, only better or more efficiently, is no longer a sufficient function of the academic dean. Deans as educational leaders at institutions facing the challenges in the *transformation age* must be agents of transformative change who engage their institutions in redefining the nature of education, its institutions, its models, and, its new place in the context of higher education, religious life, and society.

Depending on the context, a dean may be in more than one of these roles. In the liminal age of transformative change, schools need deans who can lead their institutions from what they have been to what they will need to become.

- With which of the four functions are you most personally comfortable? Steward, advocate, sponsor, or agent?
- Which of the four roles has been the traditional function of the dean in your school?
- Which of the four roles does your institution most need of a dean at this time?
- The four roles are not mutually exclusive. Can you identify to what extend you fill each role?
- Are the roles that define your function related to change dictated, limited, or supported in your school by its culture? Policies? Structure?
- Have you made a definitive shift from one role to another related to change in your context?

[1]Dale W. Lick, "Leadership and Change," in R. M. Diamond, ed. *Field Guide to Academic Leadership*. A publication of the National Academy for Academic Leadership. Jossey-Bass, 2002, p. 29.

❖

The Dean Creates the Right Kind of Change

At a conference on leadership I was again struck by how the level of energy (anxiety?) in the room increased when the topic focused on change. This is natural, of course, since one of the critical functions of leaders, including deans, is to bring about positive change on several levels. In fact, it is likely that a new dean will begin her or his term of office with a mandate to make changes in the system----notwithstanding that any attempts of consequence to do so on his or her part of the leader will likely meet with resistance if not outright sabotage.

The resistance to change is natural in that the nature of emotional process in any system includes the force of homeostasis. Homeostatic dynamics resist change at the most fundamental levels: those that upset the balance of dynamics that have established patterns of relationships, structures of influence, and those systemic structures and processes that inform identity (like culture and practices).

It can be helpful for school deans to not only understand the nature of change in organizations, but to discern the type of change needed during a particular stage in the life of the school. Deans are well served to understand the nuances in understanding the types and levels of change necessary and possible. An important question for the dean is, "what kind of change am I trying to bring about in my school at this time?" The list below depicts different kinds of change according to their level from easy to bring about to harder to achieve. From top to bottom these levels of change take a short time to bring about (e.g., programmatic) to a long time to realize (e.g., cultural and evolutionary). The lower on the list the type of change the more it is a type of "fundamental" or "adaptive" change.

TYPES OF CHANGE

Programmatic
Administrative
Organizational
Structural
Cultural
Developmental
Evolutionary

Change at any level invites anxiety if not reactivity. However, change at the more fundamental level often is perceived as threat, so deans should expect a higher level of reactivity and resistance to the change. Depending on the resilience of the system, change at any level may bring a minimal or a great deal of anxiety and reactivity. Systems with a low tolerance for change can experience major crises with attempts at even benign programmatic changes.

Few remain in the office of the dean long enough to bring about change at the more essential levels, those that impact developmental or evolutionary change, which shifts the emotional process in the system, including homeostasis. The typical tenure of most deans is five to seven years. This has dire implications for the health and vitality of schools living in a current age of swift technical changes, drastic cultural changes, and multiple external stressors. My hunch is that the schools that will service and thrive over the course of the next two decades are those who can be resilient enough to embrace change at the more fundamental levels while maintaining their core mission. The role of the dean as an agent of change will be a critical factor in this.

Deans, who lead from the center, need to discern the right kind of change needed for right time. To mistake programmatic change for developmental change is a potentially costly blunder. To force organizational change in an attempt to bring about cultural change will ultimately be ineffective.

Effective deans know the type of change they need to bring about, and they understand the processes necessary to realize those changes, including, dealing with resistance and sabotage. Of course, seasoned deans also know not expect to hear, "Thank you for all these changes you are making around here."

❖

The Dean and Cultural Change

One of the most important functions deans provide for their schools is helping to shape the culture of the school. Changing a culture is also one of the most difficult things to do. Steve Denning, author of *The Leader's Guide to Radical Management*, explained that, "...an organization's culture comprises an interlocking set of goals, roles, processes, values, communications practices, attitudes and assumptions. The elements fit together as an mutually reinforcing system and combine to prevent any attempt to change it." Deans work on changing the culture from the position as second chair leader in their areas of influence. In many ways the position of the first chair leader (e.g., President) facilitates changing the culture easier than it is for the second chair.

As dean I only had influence in the corners of the institution for which I was directly responsible. Being good with boundaries, did not address directly other areas in the institution, though given the interlocking nature of complex organizations, all areas to some extent impacted my office and its work. When I was first chair at the school at which I was Principal, changing the culture was a lot easier. As first chair I set the tone, defined the values, and could make critical decisions to address liabilities. For example, I fired three persons my first year out of the need to establish a culture of accountability. One resource I had in that context was "the power of the paycheck" (something not available to most deans). But firing the under-performers only helped the solid people function better. And holding people accountable ultimately made for a healthier system.

Changing the culture means changing institutional values as well as corporate practices and behaviors. Defining those values that need to be cultivated and embodied through practices, behaviors, attitudes and demeanor is key. Once you identify those, you have to repeat them 1000 times, call them out when you see them, and provide correctives as necessary. The goal is to get the system to the place where everyone knows "the way we do it here," or, "This is what we do and how we do it because this is who we are."

Deans, with their Presidents, must take the lead in changing the culture. They set the tone, communicate expectations, and embody the cultural values they want to inculcate into the system. There will be resistance, but people in the system will follow.

From my perspective, here examples of values and behaviors that foster a healthy culture:

- Increased professionalism: decorum, graciousness, consideration, and effectiveness (one can be "cool" and professional).
- Practices of accountability. This includes a "no excuses" attitude for the things persons have responsibility for getting done. The function of educational assessment fits here.
- Cultivation and practice of transparency. Organizations need to trust their leaders. One can be brutally honest while being gracious.
- The practice of spiritual graces, like piety, hospitality, and humility. This is a critical cultural facet for seminaries preparing persons for ministry. "Formation" of clergy is more caught than taught.
- An expectation and demand for excellence.

- Promote, perpetuate, or reshape the narrative. Leaders need to "tell the story" of the system, often. But, leaders can re-shape and re-interpret the narrative. For example, re-shaping the narrative can involve telling "we used to be...., but now we are...."

The task of academic deans is varied. Some days, it can seem we're responsible for just about everything in the system. And while these tasks are all important, none will be as far reaching in impact and significance than in the dean's capacity to shape a school's culture.

❖

The Dean and Organizational Change

Bringing about organizational change isn't rocket science, but it's not easy either. Those deans who step into a leadership position that requires engaging in institutional and organizational development, in effect and by default, will need to bring about changes on several levels: administrative, cultural, organizational, relational, and in processes and structures. In other words, institutional development is systemic. It requires addressing change in everything all together at the same time.

One aspect of bringing about institutional change is problem solving, and that skill is a major part of the game. Every change brings about a potential new problem. And that problem needs to be solved. For problem solving I know of few things more helpful than the Feynman Problem Solving Algorithm. I've found that if I follow it rigorously and to the letter it works every time:

The Feynman Problem Solving Algorithm:

1) Write down the problem.
2) Think very hard.
3) Write down the solution.

A second more helpful list comes from John Champlin who identified critical factors for bringing about effective change in an institution. They include:

- The creation and support of clear, attainable goals that are publicized and constantly in use
- The presence of a change agent who can effectively break the equilibrium (homeostasis) holding an organization in place
- The use of a systematic, planned process that is open and subject to alteration
- The involvement of the community as an active partner and participant in any major change
- The presence of effective leadership with vision, a sense of mission, a goodly measure of courage, and a sense of the importance of the mission
- A commitment to renewal that disallows compromising for lesser attainments and always aspires to higher levels of sophistication.

Do you have a framework for interpreting and guiding organizational change in your school?

Have you published your goals for the changes needed in your school?

How effective are you in soliciting and attracting support from others to help bring about change?

Do you challenge the key members of your organization to higher standards of behavior and performance?

❖

20 Ways the Dean Can Say "No"

Deans sometimes have a tough time saying "No." Many just need to be liked too much and no one wants to be seen as the resident Scrooge who is miserly with resources. Yet, there is no end of requests that come across the dean's desk.

It's not uncommon for a dean to be assaulted by an enthusiastic staff or faculty member with an idea for a new initiative or a perceived need in the hallway between office and coffee room, or, between the faculty lounge and class. But, deans do need to say "No" when appropriate. If they hang around the job long enough most deans will develop a tough enough skin to say "No" relatively easy. Others develop a more delicate and politically palatable manner for staying off pleas for privileges, exceptions, or personal projects. The trick, of course, is to sound sincere and provide a rationale that is believable enough to not be questioned overmuch. Or, hopefully, to postpone the issue long enough for the petitioner to lose interest.

Here are twenty ways deans can say "No" that can serve as a stay against requests you don't want to entertain:

- We didn't budget for that.
- Maybe if we get a grant we can do that.
- The President won't go for it.
- The Trustees won't like it.
- The accreditation committee won't allow for that.
- It's not in the by-laws.
- There's no room for that in the course rotation schedule.
- We don't have the right size faculty to do that.

- We don't have a large enough student FTE for that.
- We'd have to hire more staff for that.
- The Faculty committee that would need to handle that no longer exists.
- The Faculty Manual (or Academic Manual, or Personnel Manual) may not allow that; I'll have to check.
- That does not fall within the degree program goals.
- We don't have a rubric for that.
- Can you draw up a proposal for that?
- That will put you over the teaching load.
- It's in the budget, but we don't have the money.
- Let's wait till after the curriculum revision is done.
- Let's wait till after the accreditation visit is over.
- I think we need to leave that for the next dean.

Despite the tongue-in-cheek list, saying no isn't always easy, but it is often necessary. Sometimes we fear people won't like our decision. Other times we fear people won't like us because of our decision. But both are beside the point in the job deans must do.

Deans are stewards of a wide ranging area within their institutions, covering multiple facets with limited resources. Few in the organization have the vantage of position that gives them the capacity to see how saying "yes" to one thing impacts other areas in positive and/or potentially negative ways. For deans, saying "No" just comes with the job.

❖

When Faculty Members Misbehave

Times of high anxiety tend to bring out reactivity. There's no question we're living in anxious times, and schools are not exempt from the stress or threats of the era. In anxious times deans and administrators can expect to see an increase in the number of cases of employees or faculty members "behaving badly." One common lament among hapless leaders is, "I don't understand how they can act that way!"

When faced with reactivity in the form of bad behavior we often are taken aback about how adults can act badly. The mistake, of course, is in seeking a rationality behind bad behavior. There is no "reasoning" or rational to emotional reactivity. Therefore, it's of little value to question people's motives for bad behavior. But it is worth asking, "Hmm, I wonder where that came from?"

Generally, there are four goals for bad behavior: getting attention, gaining power, getting revenge, and covering up feelings of inadequacy. Because reactivity is a function of emotionality, reactive bad behavior has as a goal soliciting an emotional response from others. This is why it is important for leaders to be able function from a thinking posture and *respond* to reactivity, rather than *react* to reactivity. That is easier said than done, of course. Leaders benefit from learning to operate at a different level than the anxious flux in the emotional field when in the midst of reactivity. Mentally asking, "What's really going on here?" is a helpful technique for getting below the surface of bad behavior.

The chart below identifies the goal of the bad behavior, the anxiety it addresses, identifies the response it seeks, and suggests the corrective response needed.

The Four Goals of Bad Behavior

	Getting Attention	**Gaining Power**	**Getting Revenge**	**Covering up Inadequacy**
Goal of behavior	Getting attention, being acknowledged	Wants to be in control.	Desires to hurt others.	Wants to hide, avoid demands and responsibilities
Typical functioning	Being a nuisance, showing off, clowning, underfunctioning.	Acting stubborn, arguing, tantrums, lying, passive-aggressive behavior, underfunctioning.	Projects own hurt feelings onto others. Defiant, sullen, sore loser, delinquent behavior.	Feels inferior, gives up, and rarely participates, talks a good game but does not follow through, clowning.
Anxiety addressed	Being ignored is to be insignificant.	Feels secure when they can control others.	Getting even with people is the only hope to be achieved.	Fear that others will discover how inadequate they feel/are.
Emotional response sought	Annoyance, acknowledgement. Solicits overfunctioning on the part of others.	Defeated, threatened, provoked. Power struggles.	Hurt feelings, outrage, retaliation, conflict, feuding.	Abandonment, neglect so that they'll be left alone.
Corrective response	Do not reward neediness. Being punitive or demonstrating annoyance is a reward. Only provide attention or acknowledgement when this person does something positive.	Avoid power struggle. Reversals (give them the power they think they want). Join the resistance. Demonstrate respect as appropriate. Ask for their help.	Do not demonstrate hurt feelings or frustration. Provide consequences, but not punishment. Reversals. Provide encouragement when appropriate.	Encouragement, praise for effort. Don't give up on them. Challenge. Do not cater to their weakness.

It can be helpful for a leader to appreciate that while there is no "reason" for bad behavior, there is a *cause* behind people's reactivity expressed in the form of bad behavior. Bad behavior serves a purpose. Some people engage in bad behavior because they intuitively understand the purpose the bad behavior will serve. Others engage in reactivity as a learned behavior that yields a desirable response from others. This is not unlike the three-year-old who has learned that throwing a tantrum will help him get his way.

One fascinating insight is that these behaviors hold true for children and adults. In children the behavior is often easier to recognize, but the same dynamic, and motives, applies for adults. The reason for this is people do not easily change their emotional repertoire over the course of their lives. When we encounter adults acting badly and find ourselves asking, "How can they act that way?" it may be helpful to realize that we're observing an emotionally functional ten-year-old.

We can allow people their right to go insane every once in a while. When overcome by anxiety, any of us will get reactive. Persons whose pattern it is to act out irresponsibly to get attention, gain power, or attain revenge, however, should be called on it. As for persons who consistently act out of feelings of inadequacy, the rule for the leader is to not cater to, encourage, or promote weakness.

❖

"Sharecropper" by Israel Galindo. Graphite on paper 9"x11"

Deaning from the Right Side of the Brain

I have been a lifelong doodler. In fact, my college class notes look more like sketchbooks than notebooks (and the doodles are the only reason I've kept some of my college notes). Even today pencil and sketchpad are not far from reach in the event an idle moment provides opportunity to doodle. At times doodles have turned into sketches. The graphite drawing below, done several years ago, started as a doodle that eventually became a favorite sketch, which today hangs framed in my study.

People sometimes say, "Wow, how do you do that?" On occasion my playful reply is, "Well, if you do something every day for most of your life you can get pretty good at it." Drawing helps artists develop a way of seeing things different than most non-drawing people seem able. Artist and teacher Brian Bomeisler was featured in *American Artist* magazine.[1] Bomeisler (the son of Betty Edwards, author of the best seller *Drawing on the Right Side of the Brain*)[2] teaches the "Global Skills of Drawing" that help students produce more realistic drawings. In effect, he teaches them the principles that help them see the world as it is as opposed to seeing the world as they assume it is.

The global skills of realistic drawing Bomeisler teaches include these five skills:

1. The perception of edges called line or contour drawing.
2. The perception of spaces in drawing called negative spaces.
3. The perception of relationships known as perspective and proportion.
4. The perception of lights and shadows called shading.
5. The perception of the whole, which comes from the previous four perceptual skills.

All five of Bomeisler's skills of "realistic drawing" are applicable to the work of the school dean, which sometimes, seems to require as much art as it does skill. Each of those concepts has a corollary when it comes to leadership in the school context. I like the corollary because, as deans, one of our tasks in academic leadership is to understand the culture of our schools and how its context affects all those involved: faculty, students, administration, staff, and the churches we serve.

1. Deans need to develop a perception of edges called "boundaries."

One important concept for deans is differentiation in relationship systems. The concept involves knowing where one's boundary of self (which includes our personal identity, thinking, feelings, and responsibilities) ends and another's begins. People who lack a perception of boundaries tend to have a larger pseudo-self than a core self. In times of acute anxiety and reactivity persons who lack the right perception of boundaries can become willful and invasive. A lack of boundaries can also lead to overfunctioning behaviors (and overfunctioning is always willful).

Conversely, lacking capacity for differentiation can leave a dean incapable of settling boundaries when others are invasive, demanding, or seductive. Effective deans not only understand boundaries, they are able to set them when needed. For example, healthy deans know the boundaries between the need to service the curricular needs of the school, and the desires and preferences of faculty members. Emotionally mature deans know the boundaries between personal self (one's identity) and the pseudo-self (e.g., the "role" of dean) that is appropriately shared with the school system. Further, effective leaders know how to draw a line in the sand when dealing with willful persons who lack respect for boundaries.

2. Deans need to develop a perception of what they cannot see, like "negative spaces."

We can relate this point to the capacity to perceive emotional process in the system. You can't see emotional process directly, but you can see its effect on the system and in the individuals that make up the system. Emotional process is the driving force that makes anxious people do what they do when they engage in automatic responses. It is the force that fuels reactivity and the power behind homeostasis. I define emotional process as, "The patterned ways in which an emotional system facilitates the dynamics through which relationships are developed and function in order to maintain homeostasis."

Being able to see the "negative space" of emotional process is the ability to focus on how people function in a system, rather than focusing on individual personalities or secondary characteristics (like gender, race, ethnicity, cultural heritage, or what academic area that person teaches). Leading from "the right side of the brain" yields the ability to perceive an episode of reactivity in the context of the emotional process in the school system (including its cultural and institutional history), as opposed to interpreting it as an isolated instance in time. It is the ability to recognize triangulation when you see it (or when you're in it) and being able to discern your place in the triangle and the forces that put you there merely by virtue of being the dean.

3. Deans need to develop a perception of relationships.

If deaning is about anything, it is about leadership through the influence of relationships. One of the most transformative moments in deaning happens when deans, as leaders, can re-frame their perception about their relationship with their school and become the positive deviant in the system: that person who can be in the system yet perceive the flow and flux of the emotional process that affects persons within the system. Gaining a new perspective on the nature of leadership and of relationships can be freeing, if not redemptive, especially for those caught in the trap of transferring their own family of origin emotional process issues and patterns onto their work in the position of dean. We tend too quickly to fall into the trap of functioning as if leadership is about control, ensuring results, getting people to do things, or managing an organization. For deans, leadership, in contrast, is about influence rather than control, integrity rather than results, enabling persons to do their best work, and working toward organizational and institutional effectiveness.

4. Deans need to develop the perception of shading.

Moving away from either/or and right-or-wrong thinking is key to better leadership functioning. The power of leading from "the right side of the brain lies in the ability to engage in imagination. Being able to work with a broad palate of hues and tones of grays, rather than just in black and white, can help the academic deans and administrators entertain options beyond the fight or flight reactivity that is brought on by anxiety in times of crises. The ability to perceive the reality of tones, hues, and shades can help in relationships also. It will help the dean see people in a new light and appreciate that all humans are complex, nuanced, multidimensional, and wonderfully made. It can help deans move beyond the temptation to over simplistically ascribe motives to puzzling behaviors and can help them appreciate the influence of emotional process on people's function—a process which they themselves often are unaware. The way people function, think, and feel are colored as much by their family of origin, sibling position, emotional maturity, ability to self-regulate, beliefs, and level of differentiation as they are by "motives" or cognition.

5. Deans need to develop a perception of the whole.

Developing the capacity to "think systems," to see the whole rather than the individual parts is critical to deans and administrators. Like an artist who can see the whole canvas and envision how all aspects of composition help bring balance and proportion to the whole, deans need to see the system's patterns, relationships, dynamics, and forces—rather than merely their effects on its particular objects. Often, it is not what is on the foreground that's most interesting—it is the rest of the components in the "field" that are making us focus on the object of interest that are the most dynamic forces at play. For school deans the "field" that makes up the whole includes the position of his or her school within the landscape of education, and, the broader field of higher education, something most others in the school system will likely not see as part of their work, nor realize the influences of those broader interconnected systems.

For example, examine the sketch "Sharecropper." If you look carefully you will note that the composition of the sketch uses the classic "triangle" to force the viewer's gaze toward the eyes of the subject—the viewer cannot help but focus there. But since the "triangle" is part of the composition, which is hidden to the eye, most viewers will not be aware of what the "field" of the sketch is forcing them to look at. Deans are most effective when they understand "what is really going on" and know how to perceive what others cannot. The capacity of the dean to gaze beyond the horizon line, and see what others cannot, is what we call vision. Changing our way of seeing in order to develop persistence of vision is hard work. But, like doodling, if you do it every day for a long time, you can get pretty good at it.

[1] You can read the article at: http://www.myamericanartist.com/2007/02/drawing_without.html
[2] Betty Edwards, *Drawing on the Right Side of the Brain* (Los Angeles, California: J.P. Tarcher, 1989).

❖

The Dean as Positive Deviant

Albert Einstein has been quoted as saying, "Few people are capable of expressing with equanimity opinions which differ from the prejudices of their social environment. Most people are even incapable of forming such opinions."

Every organization does well to avoid the trap of shaping its perception of reality based on self-referencing. By self-referencing I mean believing its own myths, spin, and PR narrative, and, believing that their culture is normative and universal to their field or business. No institution is as great as it tends to believe itself to be; nor, often, is it as bad off as it may think. There are two elements that can provide correctives to the trap of self-referencing. First, there is the practice of rigorous institutional formative assessment that allows data to provide the framework for interpretation and decision-making. The second is less common but potentially has greater potential for change and development: the presence of a positive deviant in a position of influence in the organization.

The concept of a positive deviant comes from behavioral scientist Gretchen Spreitzer, clinical professor of management and organizations, and Scott Sonenshein. They define positive deviance as "intentional behaviors that significantly depart from the norms of a referent group in honorable ways." They explain, "Positive deviance focuses on those extreme cases of excellence when organizations and their members break free from the constraints of norms to conduct honorable behaviors." Spreitzer says, "It has profound effects on the individuals and organizations that partake and benefit from such activities."[1]

By virtue of the position of second chair leader, academic deans can potentially serve as positive deviants in their institutions. Perhaps because deans lead from the center and have cast a wide field of influence within the school, they have great potential to function as resident positive deviant than others in the organization. Given the challenges schools face in the wake of the systemic changes in the field of education and uncertainties in society and its institutions in the current age, a resident positive deviant can help a school break from the stuckness that leaves it unable to respond to challenges with imagination and resilience.

Spretzer and Sonenschein posit three criteria for positive deviance: voluntary behaviors; significant departure from the norms of a referent group; and honorable intentions. Positive deviants depart substantially from norms, and by their actions improve organizational functioning by helping it get beyond the "we've never done it that way" syndrome and the failure of critical self-reflection.

What may be ways deans can be positive deviants in their organizations?

- Maintaining the integrity of the mission while reinventing the models and practices that interpret it
- Honoring the institutional heritage while moving the institution along its liminal historical trajectory
- Helping to articulate the vision for the school's' next incarnation
- Helping the school evaluate conduct (that ought or ought not to occur) with a view to understanding the expectations and assumptions that underlie their practice
- Challenging complacency while fostering excellence and accountability
- Cultivating appreciation and encouragement for innovation, imagination, and experimentation
- Fostering a shift in loyalty from individual preferences, predilections and need to the welfare of the school for the benefit of all
- Pushing past tendencies of anxiety-motivated desires for safety to taking responsible risk

- Expanding beyond a parochial and local perspective to a more global stance
- Interpreting the local situation within the larger context (e.g., the school is situated in the context and industry of higher education; the school can have influence on global issues)
- Envisioning where the institution needs to be in five years and doing now the things needed to get there.

As leaders of influence standing at the center of the organization, deans can provide prophetic vision and strategic direction when they cultivate the stance of resident positive deviant.

1Gretchen M. Spreitzer and Scott Sonenschein, "Toward the Construct Definition of Positive Deviance," *American Behavioral Scientist* (Vol. 47, Issue 6. February 2004).

❖

Leading From the Center

Jeanne P. McLean's seminal work on the role of the academic dean as an act of "leading from the center" is apt and resonates with those of us who have experienced the job. But in the whirlwind of the experience of leading form the center, one may well ask, "the center of what?"

Schools in higher education carry on their work at the intersection of at least three spheres of influence, and the dean resides at the center of that intersection. The three primary spheres of influence are: (1) the academic guilds of which faculties are a part; (2) the field of higher education, including the accrediting agencies; and (3) the matrix of constituents, professions, fields, networks, and industries to which their students are related. These three spheres of influence both support and compete for the school in which the dean carries out her or his work. At times these areas compete against the school for resources, loyalties, and ideologies. Furthermore, among them, the three spheres of influence may have conflicting interests, leaving the dean feeling like he or she is "caught in the middle."

The specific context and mission of a particular school will, to some degree, determine to what extend each sphere of influence is dominant. In some contexts the academic guild and scholarship may be overwhelmingly influential in the school's culture, Faculty ethos, and mission. In another the influence of industries and constituents may exert influence above that of scholarship, or even, of academic achievement. It may be that academic achievement, or scholarship, or practical leadership preparation, may be a preeminent concern depending on the school's mission and the expectations, if not demands, or its constituents. Over time a dean may experience the influence of one sphere wane while another takes precedence. Certainly when re-accreditation visits loom close on the calendar, the concerns of accrediting bodies becomes the predominant focus for a school.

For some schools, arguably, the most significant spheres of influence are, in order: (1) the influence of the academic guilds through the presence and work of Faculty in the school's culture and its influence on the curriculum; (2) the influence of the field of higher education related to institutional organization, validation, and legitimacy; and lastly, (3) the influence of the constituents the school purportedly exists to serve. Representative players from within those spheres of influence are the direct concern of the academic dean, who must balance the stewardship of the office, and the resources of the schools, with the demands of each.

So, the dean is at the center, but at the center of what? As McLean noted," While these spheres of responsibility are not unrelated, each has its own distinct and considerable demands. At this center where activities converge, the stresses and frustrations, the challenges and possibilities of the deanship reside."[1]

FRUSTRATIONS

Within this framework, deans can face multiple frustrations:

- The demands of Faculty to give preeminence and make accommodations for personal pursuits of scholarly activities (sabbaticals, time away from teaching in the classroom, etc.)
- The demands of the administration to keep the school viable and work with limited resources.
- The demands of business leaders for accountability, or for accommodation of perceived or actual needs of industries
- The demands of social leaders to highlight and address certain issues (social justice, etc.)
- The demands of students to accommodate, well, just about anything.
- The demands of business leaders to produce graduates fully prepared for the complexities of the real world.
- The demands of accrediting bodies to demonstrate compliance on multiple concerns, many of which consume resources that may rob the institution from focusing on its primary mission.

CHALLENGES

Given the reality of leading from the center, and being in a position of needing to address all spheres of influence to some extent, deans face certain challenges few in the organization do.

- Holding to the integrity of the work of the school given the competing voices and concerns that influence the system.
- Appreciating the perspectives and speaking the language of the constituents from the three fields of influence.
- Interpreting the significance and valid concerns of each field to the constituents of the others.

- Interpreting the work of the school to constituents in each sphere with transparency and integrity.
- Navigating the cloudy intersections the fields of influence create in the space the dean resides.
- Presiding as chief academic officer working to ensure students are prepared for the work of their field in a context that is better designed to prepare academics and students to be, well, academics and students.

Deans do lead from the center, as Jeanne McLean rightly described. It is important for deans, however, to once in a while take stock of where they are situated and ask themselves the question, "From the center of what?"

Which field is most influential in your context?
Which field of influence most informs your work?
Which field of influence demands most attention of you?

In which field of influence are you most comfortable leading?
Is there one field you tend to neglect?
Is there a "balance" that needs to be achieved among the three competing fields in your context?

[1]Jeanne P. McLean, *Leading From the Center: The Emerging Role of the Chief Academic Officer in Theological Schools* (Atlanta: Scholars Press, 1999).

❖

Everything Takes Five Years

I am often reminded of what my friend Margaret Macuson, author of *Leaders Who Last*, says about bringing about change in congregations, which is, "Everything takes five years."[1] While that's a bit tongue-in-cheek, it's not far from the truth. Over the past several years I've had casual conversations with many deans and leaders related to how long it takes to get things done in their organizations. Each highlighted a different aspect of the dynamic.

Gaining trust takes time. A conversation with one dean highlighted how long it takes for folks to learn to trust a new leader. Trust is not something that is given totally by virtue of position or office. And if we've followed a leader who has not left well, then gaining trust can be even more difficult. Gaining people's trust takes about five years.

Flushing the system takes time. One recent graduate, only two years out of school, is leaving her first professional position. She's feeling frustrated that people on her teams don't seem to listen to her ideas, don't seem to take her seriously and don't follow her leadership. I shared with her my own perspective that in order to begin to get things done you sometimes have to "flush the system" first. That is, you have to transition out the people currently in place that you inherited and start putting in the people you want. Getting the people you want in the right places takes about five years.

Learning the culture takes time. My conversation with a pastor revealed his surprise at how long it took for him to understand some of his church's behaviors and practices. He is in his sixth year of ministry in the congregation and only now is becoming aware of some of the history behind issues, practices, and habits. For one thing, he's noticing that church members are starting to share a different kind of information, one that includes history, stories, and "insider" knowledge that they hadn't shared before. It takes about five years to begin to understand the culture.

Getting settled takes time. I recently met with an organization' leadership team for a consultation. When I began soliciting basic information about their organization I asked how long their boss had been there. When they said, "Six years," I said, "O.k., so he's been here long enough to have survived a couple of crises and for you to suspect he's going to stay." That got a huge laugh from the group; they recognized the truth in the statement. Later I stressed that at six years, the leader was in the position "to begin to start" making plans and dreaming about what the organization's vision can be. Getting settled takes about five years.

Successful leadership requires cultivation and development of the organization. Everything takes five years. Sadly, I suspect that too many impatient deans and administrators don't take the long view and end their tenures before they can even begin to start to make a difference. Too often the first crisis (right around the third year) is seen as a personal attack or a personal failure, rather than something that is a matter of course. The key is to get through it and beyond it. The tenacity that can help the dean come out on the other side of the first crisis is what often facilitates the capacity to bring about change.

[1]Margaret Marcuson, *Leaders Who Last: Sustaining Yourself and Your Ministry* (Seabury Books, 2009).

❖

The Nine Best Ways to Ruin Your Staff

For those academic leaders, deans and administrators, who want to keep and develop quality staff colleagues, here are the ten most common ways supervisors ruin their staff—and how to avoid them. (For those who *want* to get rid of troubling staff, then this is the way to do it!).

1. **Demand perfection and conformity.** Insecure leaders tend to demand unrealistic expectations. If you are a secure leader, however, you will seek out mature and competent staff and free them to carry out their work. You will learn from them — they will be good teachers to you, challenge you, and be colleagues (I often tell associate staff that "Job 1" of any staff specialist is to educate the boss). If you get a novice staff member, then remember that you'll be doing a lot of on-the-job training. Part of your job then, is to be a mentor. That's a call to stewardship related to the profession.

Let your staff make their own mistakes and remember that their mistakes and failures along the way are not a reflection on you. Pastoral ministry is not science, it is relationship. Staff relationships take a long time to cultivate and along the way, it will be messy.

2. **Micromanage and overfunction.** Insecure leaders tend toward being willful and lack an ability to respect boundaries. Those tendencies manifest themselves in overfunctioning, herding and groupthink. Overfunctioning leaders take responsibility for what is not theirs. They take on others' anxiety and impose themselves on their staff: micromanaging their work, setting their schedules, and thinking for them. For example, they'll constantly ask for the numbers (then offer pointed suggestions for increasing the statistics), insist on unrealistic office hours, set program goals for staff members (often without the staff member's consultation), or, make staff members responsible for other people's functioning.

Effective leaders treat their staff like professionals, knowing that staff will rise to the leader's level of expectations, but more importantly, they will rise to the level of the example the leader sets. Effective leaders allow their staff to shape their ministry—it's what they were called to do.

3. **Divide and conquer.** Insecure leaders tend to play a game of divide and conquer with their staff. Fearful of losing control or influence they are not able to develop their staff into a team of colleagues. They engage in secrecy, sharing information with some individuals on staff while withholding it from others. The result is that staff members never really know what's going on and become perpetually territorial. Effective leaders realize that specialization does not mean compartmentalization. The best staff members are team players and they understand that the work and mission belongs to all of them together, not separately. Effective leaders work at cultivating a team of colleagues by developing trust through honesty. They appreciate that a strong staff team is their primary resource for ministry leadership.

4. **Do not plan together.** There is no better way to isolate staff members and fail to develop a shared staff culture than to fail to do planning together. I remain amazed at the number of leaders who do planning in isolation, or, assign it as a task to a specialist staff member.

There are few ways as meaningful and effective for developing a strong staff than to participate in planning the mutual work in which they are involved. Here are some of the benefits of doing so:
- It provides an opportunity for staff members to spend time together
- It cultivates a shared corporate ownership of the mission
- It taps into the talent and expertise that each staff member can contribute to shaping the central activity of the work
- It helps foster the development of a staff culture, with shared values, perspectives, and practices.

5. **Maintain a dysfunctional staff environment.** Tolerating a dysfunctional staff environment results in an eventual crisis of such proportion that resolution becomes impossible. In many cases a supervisor's failure to cultivate a highly functioning staff results in tolerating mediocrity in staff members.

Effective leaders cultivate the resources that foster health and responsibility in the organization. They challenge their organization to hold its staff accountable, and they encourage all to aim for high standards.

6. **Make staff members responsible for other people's functioning.** A sure sign of reactivity and anxiety is when supervisors start making staff members responsible for the functioning or behavior of others. One of the things that most frequently brings staff members to a coaching session with me is when the boss has triangled them in this manner.

Effective leaders understand that staff members are responsible for the stewardship of their own work, not for the decisions or functioning of others in the organization.

7. **Lower your expectations and your standards.** I am constantly taken aback at the low expectations organizations, and their leaders, seem to hold for their staff members. Too many organizations seem to have the mentality that they do not deserve, or are unable, to get the best persons out there. So, they take the attitude of "settling" for whomever they get.

Effective leaders cultivate the perspective that their organization deserves the best, and therefore, they choose the best staff. There is no valid reason for settling for and tolerating mediocrity in the organization and among staff. If you accept lower standards and tolerate mediocre performance from staff, you'll lose your best people first. That said, here are some things to keep in mind:

- Experience counts (most of the time), but personal maturity counts for more. When seeking good staff, I'd choose personal maturity over experience almost every time.
- Invest in the long-term (it takes three years to get competent at any job). A string of short-termed staff tenures gets you nowhere.
- Supervisors who set high standards for their staff members need to function at a high level of competence and professionalism themselves. There are fewer ways to lose the respect of your staff than to be a poor performer and unprofessional. Set your own standards, but set them high.

8. **Neglect your own professional and personal growth**. You can only influence your staff higher performance to the extent that YOU are growing in your own professional and personal life. Organizations love overfunctioning staff, they do not mind asking staff to sacrifice their families and health on the altar of the work. The dean or administrator must set the example for stewardship of one's vocation and personal life. Modeling ways to invest in your own personal growth, professional development, and self care can empower your staff to follow suit.

Additionally, here are three facts that leaders often forget related to neglecting their own care and needs. It took me ten years after I graduated with a professional degree to find my first position in my field. One factor was my determination to only accept a position that was a good "fit." The second was that it took me that long to find a leader who gave evidence that he was still working on his personal growth. In the course of ten years interviewing with organizations and their leaders I had not met one person who gave evidence of personal growth over time, participated regularly in professional development, or was able to articulate plans or activities related to a commitment to personal and professional growth.

9. Do not invest in your staff's professional development. Developing a good staff does not come about by happenstance. A collegial staff relationship can be one of the most sustaining and gratifying aspects of one's work. The reality is the leader needs to be intentional about what kind of staff he or she desires to eventually have. That requires investing in the cultivation of a good staff, including:

- Challenge your organization to develop a vision for staff (team) development
- Put money in the budget for staff development, and don't let it be the first thing to cut when there's a budget crisis
- Invest in your own professional development, it sets the example for both organization and staff
- Develop a study leave program or policy. Require of staff professional development plans.
- Read together as a staff.

Which relationships feed and challenge you in your professional life? Your relationship with your staff should be one.

Finally, here is what staff members say are the ways their supervisors can cultivate and keep a good staff:

- Provide challenge. Develop a staff culture based on shared values of excellence, commitment, responsibility and mutual accountability. Expect and demand evidence of growth,-- personal and professional, over the course of time together.
- Get your values straight, then, cultivate a common, shared value among all key persons in the organization
- Be an enabler, which is helping your staff find and work out their place in your organization

- Be a Team Leader. You are responsible for the creation and maintenance of an effective team, and, the culture that fosters it
- Be gracious and considerate in your relationship with staff, and, model what it means to be a supportive colleague
- Be a Primary Educator. This includes being a learner, investing in regular continuing education and encouraging your staff to do likewise
- Always support your staff. Value their vision and their plans. Allow them to craft and shape the ministry they were called to.
- Have a supportive spirit toward your staff. They are your colleagues, not your "hires."
- Protect them from the willful and destructive people in your organization. In the long run, leaders do well to be less fearful about losing a few troubling customers than about losing good staff.
- Never ask your staff to do things you are not willing to do yourself. And never, ever, take credit for their work.

❖

Six Challenges When Leaving Office

Most deans who are leaving office will have announced their departure from that role with a year's notice. If that's the case for you, you've turned in your graciously-worded resignation letter and the search for a new dean will begin soon. Or, perhaps, another sympathetic, possibly naive, soul from among the Faculty is waiting in the wings to take on the mantle. In either case, you'll soon start contemplating what the "last year" in office will be like, experience episodes of anticipatory grief, and maybe, occasionally closing your office door and doing the happy dance on your desk.

Regardless of the reasons for vacating the office of dean, leaving well is important. That in itself can be a great gift to an institution.

How you leave can set the tone for a smooth transition. Leaving well can help or hinder the next dean's entry, and can define your relationship with colleagues when re-entering the Faculty body. Here are five challenges when leaving office as dean:

1. Setting your pace. Some deans will move through their final year in office in "coasting" mode, marking the time until they can unburden themselves. Others will move into it with frenzied determination to get as much of the unfinished business completed before they leave office. One good rule to follow is to take responsibility for your time in office, meaning, being responsible during the last year (no slacking off). There's a balance to be struck between not defecting in place (you're still the dean), while also not trying to fix problems for the next dean, nor setting the agenda for the school for after you are out of office.

2. Navigating shifting relationships. When you took office you changed your position in the system and realigned relationships. You needed to relate differently with the President, your faculty colleagues, and the staff. Upon leaving office you will once again shift your position. You'll need to renegotiate your working relationship with all those parties, plus, the new dean, if you will remain in the school. Some will welcome you "back from the dark side" and rejoice in your redemption. Others may have difficulty re-establishing a collegial relationship with you if their experience with you as dean was prickly. This is a good time to remember the adage, "It was never about you."

3. Reentering your field of scholarship. The deanship is a full time job, and then some. If you came to the deanship from among the Faculty it probably did not take you long to figure out that you entered a different professional field than the one you trained for and practiced as teacher and academic. There's a qualitative difference between being in the field of academic leadership and administration, and practicing the scholarship of research, writing, and teaching. By your third year in office you were probably feeling a bit disconnected from your field of scholarship. The guild meetings you once attended were replaced with attendance at conferences related to accreditation, institutional compliance, organizational leadership, and training in administrative software. The pile of unread books related to your field has grown alarmingly high. You may have even canceled a favorite professional journal or two because you spent more time reading about standards, metrics, assessment, and reviewing and writing internal reports. As you leave office it is time to re-engage in the field of scholarship. Now you can get back in the game: write a journal article, dust off that book proposal, and schedule a professional conference in your field of study. Re-acquaint yourself with old colleagues and catch up on their works. Introduce yourself to the fresh-faced rising stars in your field; but you may have to convince them you were once somebody.

4. Defining your boundaries. Once you turn in your keys, you will no longer be the Dean. In another sense, however, you'll always be "dean." It's a relatively rare job, and not many hold it for long. Some will ask you for your opinion about matters, "as a dean," and you'll discover that your opinion counts for more merely by virtue of having had that position. You'll have insider knowledge about the institution, and about members in the institution, that you will need to keep confidential. You'll need to live into the challenge of setting appropriate boundaries, especially if you remain at the same institution. You are no longer the Dean, and you need to be clear about that.

5. Letting go. After you leave office you will no longer be part of the "inner circle" of decision makers. It will likely feel strange, if not unsettling, to no longer be "in the know" about what is happening in the institution. While your opinion as a faculty member may count for more than previously, your sphere of influence will be narrower. Letting go of the job may include letting go of how others define you as "the former dean." You may be praised as "a great dean," or blamed for every problem and inconvenience in the system--neither of which will be completely true. (When I left office, I told the new dean to be sure to blame me for every problem he faced. He needed to be the new "good guy.").

6. Maintaining the integrity of the office up to the last day. A common tendency in "lame duck" years of any administration is that of being magnanimous in making exemptions and granting favors. It is a non-too-subtle temptation related to not having to live with the consequences of those gestures. You get all the praise, and the next dean inherits all the headaches. Before you grant an exemption or favor to that faculty member who is praising you for being an understanding and flexible dean, it's worth remembering that while in office you remain the steward of the organization, and that includes honoring and enforcing policies. Maintain the integrity of the office to your last day; you will serve the institution better, and will prevent the next dean from having to deal with all the "accommodations" you made on your way out. Remember that one goal is to leave the institution better than how you found it.

❖

II. ACADEMIC ADMINISTRATION

The Dean and Assessment

Academic Deans often come from among the Faculty, and often out of academic disciplines not grounded in the field of education. While many have become effective teachers through years of classroom experience (often learning through trial and error) few acquire expertise as educators. Few, even as senior experienced faculty, teach out of a specific and intentionally ascribed educational theory that informs their teaching. Fewer, perhaps, can identify an educational philosophy that informs educational values, curricular decisions, programmatic design or approaches.

With the increasing demand for institutional, programmatic, and curricular assessment in higher education deans lacking expertise in educational administration and academic assessment find themselves challenged in providing what their schools need of their deans in those areas. In my consultations with deans facing those challenges I share two perspectives, (1) Assessment is not rocket science, but you need to know, and apply, the principles and practices of educational assessment, and (2) while you may not be an expert today, remember that you learn what you need to learn at the time you need to learn it. In other words, you can acquire the knowledge you need when you need it.

Below are general rules of assessment that may provide a perspective:

- You have to do it. It's part of what effective deans do, and must do well.
- People won't like it. But you have to do it anyway. Educational enterprises need to *actually* engage in the practice of education, and that includes rigorous assessment.
- Assessment is a practice of accountability. If we say we are educating people for their professions, we need to be able to demonstrate so.

- Assessment is one of the most useful tools for bringing about change. People will always resist change (it's a default emotional response), but at the end of the day, it's hard to argue with facts and data.
- To be effective, assessment must be rigorously applied. You must practice the science and art of assessment (there are some things you can't fake).
- Assessment is formative, it leads to effectiveness over time. The shortest curricular assessment cycle tends to be three years, so take the long view.
- Assessment is multi-faceted. E.g., direct and indirect assessment, first and second level, standardized, formative, diagnostic, summative, etc.
- Assessment does not have to be complicated (though it can be complex). Simpler is better, and often, less is more.
- Assessment is not data gathering. Assessment involves analysis, interpretation, evaluation, and action.
- Effective assessment measures against standards. Identify the appropriate metrics, industry standards (stress tests, bottom line, break even mark, ratios, etc.), accreditation standards, and touchstones against which to assess.
- Assessment never ends. It is cyclical in nature and builds upon itself.
- You don't have to assess everything at once. A staggered or cyclical schedule for formative assessment will allow for consistent coverage of critical areas.
- You don't have to assess everything. Everything is capable of being assessed, but not everything needs to be.
- Assessment works on several levels: institutional, administrative, programmatic, curricular, classroom.
- Assessment addresses multiple domains: learning, knowledge, skills, affect (attitudes and values), performance, results, outcomes.
- You need a plan for assessment, including a system and schedule for reports. If it's not documented, it didn't happen.

- Educational assessment has been around for decades, you don't have to reinvent the wheel. When you find a good idea steal it. When you develop a good practice, product or procedure, share your stuff--others can use the help.

❖

The Dean and Educational Effectiveness

Deans face increasing demands to demonstrate educational effectiveness from accrediting agencies and constituents. For many schools, and for new deans, this can seem like an imposing challenge. Demonstrating educational effectiveness falls to the office of the dean in most schools, highlighting again, that academic school deans need to be educational leaders in their contexts, not just scholars, teachers, and administrators. For many deans, this requires new ways of thinking and the development of new skills and capacities.

Educational effectiveness is simply providing evidence about the extent to which the school accomplishes its stated mission and goals. As such, educational effectiveness has less to do with activities (what we do) and more to do with outcomes (the demonstrable results of what we do). What evidences educational effectiveness is as multifaceted and complex as the enterprise of the school. One way to assess, and demonstrate, educational effectiveness is to identify the critical functions of the institution and its enterprise, and to identify the metrics that count for evidence. Identifying a specific cluster of meaningful metrics can help the dean focus on what is most important. This cluster of metrics can help the organization focus on the questions "What is most important to pay attention to that helps us know we're accomplishing what we want?"

Common Mistakes to Avoid

When developing and using metrics, avoid these common mistakes:

- Creating metrics for the sake of just having metrics. Metrics are indicators of meaningful factors.
- Formulating too many metrics, resulting in data tracking with little action.
- Lack of follow up. Metrics and assessment yield accountability. They solicit decision and action.
- Identifying and tracking metrics that do not lead to actions. This is just compiling trivia.
- Keeping metrics isolated from other critical indicators. Meaningful metrics tend to integrate with other critical factors (trends, comparison with peer schools, etc).

Below is a sample list of metrics that can provide the cluster of items one can choose for demonstrating educational effectiveness. The metrics are identified by categories for convenience, but the nature and complexity of an educational institution means that many metrics will integrate with those in other categories. Not all metrics are of equal weight, and all metrics are assessed in comparison to what they measure.

Sample Matriculation Metrics

- Full Time Equivalence (FTE): total for all programs, by degree program, by program concentrations, end-of-year trend comparisons, percentage increase or decrease, compared with head count.
- Entering class FTE yield
- Entering class as percentage of student body
- Entering class profile: by degree program, race, gender, geography, age. Trend analysis, comparison with peer schools.

- Graduates as percentage of student body
- Graduation class profile: by degree program, race, gender, debt, percentage placed, placement at time of graduation
- Student/Faculty ratio
- Average classroom enrollment
- Tuition revenue as percentage of budget
- Retention rate
- Graduation rate
- Failure to complete program tracking (dismissals, drops, factors)

Sample Academic Programs Metrics

- Enrollment in particular academic programs as percentage of enrollment
- Graduates by programs (trends)
- Enrollment in concentrations by percentages
- Student/Faculty ratio (avg class size)
- Comparative trend and impact of online and classroom courses
- Faculty course load
- Ratio of adjunctive-taught courses to faculty-taught courses
- Length of time to finish programs of study
- Grade distribution reports
- GPA (by gender, by age profile, by entering class)
- Credits taken per term (average, trend, by student profile)
- Number/percentage of courses canceled due to lack of enrollment (trend, ratio)
- Reported satisfaction with programs by current students; by alumni.

Metrics provide insight into the performance of the school, its mission, its challenges, and its needs. They should provide honest assessment, be consistent in their application, facilitate interpretation and decisions, lead to action, and provide a means for accountability.

❖

The Dean and Educational Fundamentals

During a consultation with a school I once again encountered the dilemma faced by school leaders who lack a background in the field of education. This school has been in existence for ten years; well past the "make it or break it" point for a private school. They were at a point in their institutional development where they had the luxury of taking a breath and addressing educational issues that had been long ignored in the flying-by-the-seat-of-our-pants phase. They had a new director and a new assistant director who were eager to see the school step up to a new level as an educational institution, but both lacked formal training in the field of education or educational administration. I was struck by the parallels in that scenario with several schools who are not yet in their institutional maturity stage.

My consultation with the school included the faculty, a dedicated and committed group of folks, who also were up to the challenge of taking their school to the next level. What became apparent during the process was how difficult it was for these well-intentioned folks to "think educationally" about their school enterprise. When dealing with questions about mission and vision the teachers' vision was narrow and focused on their subject areas and their classrooms. They were not able to "think educationally" globally enough to embrace the more fundamental institutional educational concerns. This situation seems akin to someone who lacks a background in music theory being unable to appreciate or "understand" a composition or performance beyond a certain level. Or, it's like the limitations faced by someone not trained as an engineer in solving certain problems. When you don't have the language or the basic concepts you don't know how to frame the right questions. Inevitably, what happens is that people go with what they know, frame the issue or problem from that perspective, and then try to address the problem by means that do no actually solve the problem.

Educational issues must be addressed through educational categories. If the problems are educational then the questions asked must be educational ones, using educational concepts, and the solutions tried must be educational ones. The administrators at the school were caught between the pragmatic realities of the institutional infrastructure and organization and lacked the language and tools to "think educationally" about the mission of the school. In other words, neither group was able to ask the educational questions that would help them make educational decisions about the direction their wanted to go with the curriculum, or the programs they wanted to offer. The best they could do was articulate general comments (we want to be the best school in the area; we want to be known as a quality school that attracts quality students; we want to prepare our students for life and work in the 21st century, and we want to set our students on fire (that last, presumably a metaphor and not literally).

Here are some of the basic educational questions that can yield educational answers to addressing educational concerns:

- What philosophy of education will inform our school's enterprise? (e.g., Pragmatism, Perennialism, Constructivism)
- What principles of learning should we use? (e.g., Discovery learning, direct instruction)
- What should be the major sources of knowledge? (e.g., textbooks, experience, experimentation, teacher's authority and expertise)
- What model of learning will we use? (e.g., specialized or generalized; traditional or progressive?)

- What guiding metaphors will we use for the curriculum? (e.g., Kindergarten, factory, community, schooling, laboratory)
- What curricular approach will we use? (e.g., curriculum as praxis, product, or process?)
- What curricular design model will we use for the curriculum? (e.g., Dick & Carey, Gerlach-Ely, Hannafin Peck, Kemp, Knirk & Gustafson, Tripp & Bichelmeyer, Indiana, Understanding by Design, etc.)
- How will we assess that our students have learned? (e.g., standardized tests, norm-referenced, criterion-referenced, developmental, mastery, understanding, application, demonstration).

These questions consist of the "fundamentals" of any educational enterprise. Deans who lead theological schools must provide informed educational expertise to their institutions. Working toward and achieving clarity and consensus about these "fundamentals" will lead to effectiveness in teaching and learning.

❖

Eight Big Ideas About Assessment

Academic leaders in schools--deans, administrators, and program directors--must ensure that their institutions demonstrate best practices of educational assessment. They must demonstrate the educational effectiveness of their curricular programs and satisfy, at least minimally, the requirements of their accrediting agencies. In other words, deans must ensure their schools demonstrate *bona fide* "industry standard" practices in assessment.

While assessment is often seen as a burden and distraction from the fundamental work of Faculty and staff, it is a critical function for any organization. In truth, assessment is part of the job, no matter what job that is within the organization. At its core, assessment is an issue of integrity. It allows a school to answer for itself, and others, "Are we actually doing what we say we are?" "To what extent are we effectively carrying out our mission?"

Assessment can help the school's leaders answer questions like, "What value do we provide to our students? Our constituents?" "Are we making the right decisions, and how do we know?" and, "Do we have the right resources and capacities to carry out our mission?"

Published data and evidence from sound assessment practices can help prospective students with questions like, "Will I get a good education at your school?" "Will I have a satisfying and positive experience?" "Will my degree be recognized and valued?"

Rigorous assessment practices and processes help answer the questions, "We like our faculty members and think they are terrific, but how effective are they at teaching, really?" "How well does our curricular program of study achieve the goals we promise to students?" "What are the strengths of our programs? What are the weaknesses?" "Are we really the good school we claim to prospective students? Can we demonstrate it?"

It is not uncommon for educational institutions to get overwhelmed and lost in their initial initiatives into more rigorous assessment activities. Commonly, most tend to do too much, attempting to put a comprehensive assessment plan in place to make up for lost time. Often, this is a result of adopting a complex assessment plan model from a more mature organization. Sometimes it's a desire to satisfy immediately every line and element from an accrediting body's standards and accreditation manual.

Below are eight big ideas on assessment that can help provide a framework for approaching the task of institutional and educational assessment:

1. You cannot improve what you do not assess. Constant improvement, increased effectiveness, and greater efficiency need to be standing goals for any institution. We want our students to learn better, our Faculty to teach more effectively, our organizations to run more efficiently, and our alumni to be demonstrably effective leaders in their fields. Wishful thinking and self-referenced public relations messages don't make those desires a reality, however. Leaders who want to improve any facet of the school's life and work need to assess it.

2. Everything that exists, exists to a certain extent, degree, or quality. Yes, anything can be assessed. Clarify what it is you are assessing or measuring and use the correct assessment method (direct or indirect assessment; quantitative or qualitative). Remember, however, that you do not have to assess everything altogether at the same time (see no. 6).

3. Goals interpret standards, objectives interpret goals, and outcomes demonstrate effectiveness. Understand the distinct categories of assessment and ensure they align with each other. Don't confuse a strategy or activity for an outcome. Don't confuse a program standard for a goal.

4. Goals are meaningless until you define how to assess them. Review your degree program goals and determine if and where you can define them in a way that can be assessed. Effective goals are expressed as "demonstrable" outcomes.

5. Publish only the program goals and outcomes you will assess. I once consulted with a school that had eight broad program goals in one degree program, with over twenty derivative outcomes! Faculty and administration were overwhelmed trying to figure out how to align the eight lofty goals and interpret how they were manifested throughout the curricular program. They were trying to accomplish too much and attempting to evaluate too many things; few of which integrated in to a coherent assessment, and even fewer aligned with the published goals.

6. What you measure must be meaningful. Avoid the temptation to assess everything---not every activity or facet of your institution or educational program is equally important. What are the "mission critical" aspects that give evidence of vitality, viability, and effectiveness? In terms of course-level assessment, follow the rule, "teach only what you will assess."

7. Assessment is not meaningful if it does not change something. Effective assessment practices "close the loop"---they change something at some level. Demonstrate and publish how your assessment practices change what you do. Remember that data do not change people's minds; ideas do---ideas that align with passion and vision. Turn your data into vision, then implement vision with strategies.

8. Assessment is a formative practice. Assessment is not a one-shot deal done in the harried and anxious anticipation of an accreditation visit. Effective schools have a culture of assessment and practice formative assessment---a process of intentional ongoing assessment that results in measured periodic improvement.

❖

Educational Concepts Every Dean Needs to Know

Academic deans wear many hats, and, depending on the context, some more than others: administrator, supervisor, assessor, policies and accreditation compliance officer, faculty cat-herder, student adviser, counselor, and maybe even resident chaplain. One primary role for the dean, however, is that of educational leader. Often, that means being the sole person in the system who thinks about the curriculum as a whole, and, who needs to "think educationally" about the enterprise of the school.

Like any other, the field of education has its technical terms and jargon. And, as with any field, it is necessary to understand basic terms and use them accurately and as precisely as possible. This ability is necessary to help the dean think like an educator. Not to put too fine a point on it, but, when it comes to educational terminology and concepts, do you know what you're talking about?

Effective teachers are always watchful for "concepts misunderstanding" among their students. That's important because misunderstandings often lead to misapplication. Below is a taxonomy of educational categories and practices. Knowing what basic educational terms mean can lead to increased clarity when discussing curriculum, identifying actions, and making decisions about teaching and learning.

You probably use some of these terms in conversation or in written communications, but, do you know what they actually mean? Can you differentiate between an educational technique and a method? What's the difference between a process and a structure? And what, exactly, is an "approach" anyway? This chart identifies common educational categories and practices. The chart flows from the bottom to top in terms of focus from broad to narrow. The bottom two categories are "foundations" (upon which educational systems and practices build) and the others fall under the category of "pedagogy." You can use this chart to (1) clarify understanding about educational practices, (2) use educational terms more accurately, (3) design or assess educational enterprises with more integrity (e.g., one's choices of methods and approaches should be congruent with one's stated educational theory and philosophy).

A Taxonomy of Educational Practices and Categories

CATEGORY	DEFINITION	EXAMPLES
Technique	A particular way of executing a method, or a subset of a method in the actual act of teaching-learning.	Question and answer, Behavior Desist, Presenting an objective, Advanced organizers, Induction (opening, transition, closing), stimulus variation
Method	A particular pedagogy or form of procedure for accomplishing the desired learning objectives.	Small group, Lecture, Reading source materials, Testing, Dialogue, Research, Socratic
Procedure	An established or formal way of doing something, a series of actions conducted in a certain order or manner. Procedures tend to be linear and logical. Certain models, processes, and methods contain *de rigor* procedurals that ensure effectiveness.	Procedure for writing a term paper: 1. Choose a subject 2. Find sources of materials 3. Gathering research notes 4. Outline the paper 5. Write the first draft 6. Edit the paper 7. Submit the paper.
Process	A series of interrelated actions or steps taken to achieve a particular end, though not necessarily a specific outcome. Processes tend to be open-ended and can be cyclical.	Project development process: Planning, Preparation, Implementation, Review, Evaluation, Planning, etc.
Format	A particular arrangement of the structure of the educational enterprise. Applies to several levels (programmatic, course, lesson, unit, etc.).	A course of study can take may formats, e.g. traditional classroom, online, seminar, independent study, tutorial
Structure	The arrangement of and relations between the parts or element of the educational Approach or educational Model.	Centralized, Open, Sequential, Cyclical, Narrative (The simplest structure for any curriculum, unit, or lesson is: beginning, middle, end.)
Model	A specific interpretive application of an educational approach. While models have broad application they tend to focus on particular ends (outcomes), contexts, disciplines, and populations	Models tend to plot on a grid matrix with emphases on the extent to which a model is: Teacher-focused to Student-centered; Teaching-focused to Learning-focused; Cognitive-focused to Affective-focused; Cognitive-focused to Skills-focused; Heuristic to Outcomes; etc.
Approach	An informed and particular way of going about the educational enterprise congruent with one's philosophical stance and informed by a particular educational theory.	Instruction, Interpretation, Dialogical Learning, Training, Praxis-Reflection, Mentoring, Sponsorship, Cohort, Apprenticeship, Transactive, Intergenerational, Field work, Discovery learning
Educational Theory	A particular, systematic and bounded interpretation of teaching and learning	Constructivism, Waldorf, Montessori, Andragogy, Behaviorist, Cognitivist, Humanist, Social, contextual, Feminist
Educational Philosophy	A particular system of thought that holds a systematic position of basic concepts such as truth, existence, reality, causality, the nature of things and persons, and freedom.	Neo-Thomism, Idealism, Pragmatism, Perennialism

Creating a High Impact Curriculum

Today, academic school deans and program directors are under greater pressure to demonstrate the effectiveness of the curriculum offered by their schools. Pity the new dean who needs to learn the esoteric language of higher education. Deans must be conversant with (if not also demonstrate competence in): metrics, demonstrable learning outcomes, norm- and criterion-referenced assessments, the use of such assessment instruments, accreditation standards, and the broader issues in higher education that impact all facets of teaching and learning, governance, administration, and educational leadership.

An essential part of the dean's work is demonstrating the appropriate application of many of the elements and practices of formative assessment and curriculum revision. More importantly, at the end of the day (or by the conclusion of an accreditation visit), deans must be able to provide evidence of "demonstrable student learning outcomes."

At the heart of all these important, and potentially overwhelming, educational issues lies a question of integrity: does your curriculum, in its course of study, do what it promises to do? One may also ask:

- Is your curriculum effective for what it is designed to accomplish?
- Can you deliver on what you promise to students and to your constituents?
- Why should a prospective student choose your curriculum over another from a similar school?
- Does your curriculum's design help bring about high impact learning for your students?

A High Impact Curriculum

Below is the finding from the American Association of American Colleges and Universities' LEAP initiative on the elements of a high impact curriculum.[1] These are "high impact" in the sense that they are directly correlated to student success. Specifically, they are demonstrated to positively impact students' retention of learning and engagement in the learning process. The high impact pedagogies identified below do not need to all exist at the same level or to the same extent across the curriculum and its courses. Some are suitable for course-level learning approaches, while others are better suited as program-level curricular components.

In no particular order, here are the ten pedagogical practices that lead to a high impact curriculum:

- First year seminars and experiences
- Common intellectual experiences (e.g., core courses, cohort learning experiences)
- Learning communities
- Writing intensive courses
- Collaborative assignments and projects
- Field Research Projects
- Diversity and Global Learning
- Service learning, community based learning
- Internships
- Capstone Courses and Projects.

It may be worth identifying which of these high impact pedagogies can be program-level student learning activities in your curriculum. For which of these may you create program-level embedded outcomes, especially those related to skills attainment and competencies? Consider how you can embed high impact pedagogies in a four-year course of study structured for Entering, Middler, and Senior level students.

- How many of these high-impact pedagogies can you identify in your programs of study?
- How many of these high-impact pedagogies are standard components of your curriculum by design? Where do they appear in the course of study?
- For those that you can identify, is there a published pedagogical rationale for their use?
- Do any of these program-level learning strategies in your curriculum have program-level assessment components?

If any are program-level components to your curriculum, to what extend are they standardized in terms of outcomes, form, standards, and assessment? (As the study states, "...these practices *must be done well*" in order for them to be effective.).

To what extent are these complex high-impact learning pedagogies integrated among the various components of your program of study? For example, to what extent are they aligned with individual courses in the curriculum and their student learning assignments and assessments?

If you use these high impact pedagogies, are they clearly aligned with the curriculum's intended learning outcomes?

[1]George D. Kuh. Association of American Colleges and Universities, High-Impact Educational Practices: What they are, who has access to them, and why they matter."

❖

What Matters In a 21st Century Curriculum?

As Chief Academic Officers school deans provide oversight for the development of an effective curriculum. They are challenged to lead Faculty to develop a course of study that can *demonstrably* prepare students for the current, and future, needs and challenges of society and industries. That's no small challenge in this liminal epoch. Deans lead institutionally conservative organizations with industrial age structures and methods in an era of globalization and rapid technological change that is characterized by volatility, uncertainty, chaos and ambiguity (or, VUCA to use the acronym created by the U.S. Military Academy to describe the world of the 21st century).

Herbert Simon believed that all professional practice is centrally concerned with what he called "design," by which he meant the process of "changing existing situations into preferred ones."[1] The dilemma is that "design" in this sense is precisely what schools do not teach well, if at all, claims Donald A. Schon in *The Reflective Practitioner: How Professionals Think in Action*.[2]

Innovative deans struggle to lead their faculties to address the changing needs of both society and students (future social and industry leaders) through the process of education delivered through a course of study, the curriculum. How do you balance the standards-driven traditional curriculum with the current, and future, realities that are being redefined, including, among others:

- The changing nature of teaching and learning in both schools and professions
- The increasingly fragile institutional structures that support higher education
- The perceived declining value of an extended formal advanced degree

- The characteristics and needs of changing student demographics
- The pressures of uncertain economic realities in educational institutions
- The impact of compliance issues from accrediting bodies
- The isoquant changes brought about by educational technologies.

One curricular tension in higher education is finding the balance between scholarship and character formation (perhaps more accurately, between "academics" and character formation). I heard one university president actually confess to an audience, "We know this is not the best way to prepare future leaders, but we do the best we can." To what extent can a scholarship-oriented Faculty help prepare students for the realities they will face in non-academic contexts of professional life and work? Can the traditional liberal arts Faculty create and pull off the curriculum needed for the 21st century? Attempts at unlinking purpose and outcomes from traditional academic contexts are not easy for a variety of reasons.

A common liability for Faculty when engaging in curriculum revision is self-referencing, believing that what it values most in scholarship is what is most important in a degree program. Scholarship is important—that's not the issue, nor the question. The question at hand is: what is needed for a 21st century curriculum? Below is information that may be helpful to consider as Faculty makes decisions about the creating a degree program relevant to the 21st century.

Trilling and Fadel, in *21st Century Skills, Learning for life in our times* (2009) cite the study from Conference Board, Partnership for 21st Century Skills, Corporate Voices for Working Families, & Society for Human Resource Management, 2006, that lists eight essential skills for the 21st century leader. They are:

- Oral and written communication
- Critical thinking and problem solving
- Professionalism and work ethic
- Teamwork and collaboration
- Working with diverse teams and partners
- Applying technology
- Leadership and project management
- Emotional Intelligence.

And from the *Journal of Religious Leadership* (vol. 10, no. 1, spring 2011), which identified six dimensions of leadership success:

- Organizational leadership
- Public leadership
- Collaborative and connected leadership
- Reconciling leadership (conflict resolution)
- Resourced leadership (understanding local history, relating personal stories with organizational theory and best practices in conflict, ongoing change dynamics, strategic planning processes)
- Learning leadership (ongoing formal and informal learning through writing, reading, reflection that guides and directs leadership in situations of change and conflict. Capacity for self-awareness and feedback from social networks).[3]

The October 25, 2003 issue of *The Economist* offered the article, "How to run a company well: Ten commandments for successful leaders." Here's the list:

1. A sound ethical compass
2. The ability to take [sic] unpleasant decisions
3. Clarity and focus
4. Ambition
5. Effective communication skills
6. The ability to judge people
7. A knack for developing talent

8. Emotional self-confidence
9. Adaptability
10. Charm.

Given these findings about what makes for effectiveness in ministry how might you lead your Faculty to explore questions like:

- Comparing these lists with our degree program goals, to what extent are we actually preparing people to succeed in ministry?
- Given the competencies listed, do we have the Faculty we need to provide a 21st century curriculum?
- How well and to what extent does our curriculum address these identified competencies and qualities?
- How well and to what extent are we able to provide for these competencies and qualities in our course of study?
- What might we need to let go in our current curriculum in order to provide for what is needed?
- What might our curricular course of study look like if these competencies became the primary degree program goals and outcomes?
- How would we need to change our program and teaching if these competencies were the basis for assessing curricular effectiveness?

[1]Herbert Simon, *The Sciences of the Artificial* (Cambridge, Mass.: MIT Press, 1972), p. 55.

[2]Donal A. Schon, *The Reflective Practitioner: How Professionals Think in Action* (Basic Books Inc., 1983).

[3]Kyle J. A. Small, "Successful Leadership in the Early Years of Ministry: Reflections for Leadership Formation in Theological Education," *Journal of Religious Leadership* (vol. 10, no. 1, spring 2011), 57.

❖

The Dean and Program Risk Assessment

The truth is, it's hard to turn down a large gift from a donor who has the best of intentions. What sounds like an exciting opportunity to a university president or a director of donor relations can quickly become a headache by the time news gets to the dean---who often will be asked to implement the vision of the donor. The dean will then need to somehow machinate a way to fulfill its intent, convince Faculty to embrace the initiative, and find some way to "just incorporate it into the curriculum." On those occasions deans will do well to help key decision makers in the system understand four issues.

1. Understand the scope of the school's mission.

Colleges and universities are situated in the field of higher education. They are degree-granting institutions of higher learning. As such, they face constraints of accrediting agencies on almost every facet of their work, from governance, to personnel, to student services, to the shape of their curricular programs. The center of gravity of a school is its curricular programs, and most institutional decisions (from student recruitment to faculty hires) will revolve around that matrix.

Collaborative grants and donor-driven partnering initiatives are increasingly popular. Most efforts at collaboration fail, however, when a school attempts to work with an affinity partner that is outside the bounds of the mission related to its degree-granting activities, regardless of good intentions. Most efforts at partnering with groups or organizations that do not directly support the narrow focus of degree-granting curricular programs will soon become a distraction or a drain on the primary mission of the school. The smaller the institution, the truer this becomes.

2. Understand and assess the potential impact of large grants.

The rule of unintended consequences is part and parcel with grant initiatives. Sometimes the unintended consequences are fortuitously serendipitous, often, they are burdensome, sometimes, they are costly. The larger the grant, the greater the challenge of sustainability beyond the life of the funding. Large grants create enlarged infrastructure, often call for new staff hires, create additional administrative oversight, and engender additional program activities that immediately compete for resources, schedules, and time.

If nothing else, the dean can help identify the ways a large grant initiative will add additional work and activities to the current work and schedules that staff and faculty already carry.

3. Understand the need for strategic planning.

Too often donor-initiated gifts are not considered sufficiently in terms of their alignment and support of the school's strategic plan. As mentioned above, large gifts, especially unexpected donor-initiated gifts with program or activity-specific requirements, may not align with the school's current strategic plan. If accepted, the dean should anticipate some level of disruption to plans and current initiatives under development. Institutions will do well to put the breaks on moving ahead too quickly with implementation of unplanned donor-initiated initiatives. Helping donors and administration see the value of a measured and strategic study and planning process to align new initiatives with the school's strategic plan will go a long way to ensure success and avoid liabilities.

4. Understand the factor of acceptable risk.

Risk is the assessment of the probability, or threat, of loss, or any other negative occurrence caused by external or internal vulnerabilities. It is the calculation of the probability that an actual return on an investment will be lower than expected.

Part of factoring risk in a new venture includes clarity about the school's capacity to avoid it through preemptive actions. Another part of identifying risk is to avoid self-referenced decision making. This happens when an organization implements new programs or initiatives based on bias and the notion that it's a good idea just because we think it is.

When considering whether or not to start a new degree program, a new concentration, a donor-initiated project, or a grant project, deans can serve their schools best by helping decision makers and influencers gain clarity about the school's mission, to give attention to alignment with strategic plans, and engage in assessing risk. The oft-quoted notion of "let's just try it and see if it works. It's o.k. if it fails," can be liberating. Some ventures, however, are too costly to warrant undue risk of failure.

The chart on the next page, "Assessment of Program Potential and Risk" can serve as a tool to evaluate new programs and ventures. A more comprehensive version can be found at:
www.wabashcenter.wabash.edu/2015/03/the-dean-and-program-risk-assessment

ASSESSMENT OF PROGRAM POTENTIAL AND RISK

Use this worksheet to assess the potential of new programs in three domains: social value potential, market potential, sustainability potential. This worksheet can be used to assess current programs or as a tool for exploring future projects, degree programs, or enterprises. Rank + or –

SOCIAL VALUE POTENTIAL (Value)	
Strategic Alignment	Program will create social value that is aligned with mission
Achievable Outcomes	Program will create a significant positive change in user behavior, condition, or level of satisfaction
Partnerships and Alliances	Partners has a synergistic effect and improve or increase chances for desired results and social value
Organizational Benefit	Successful program will increase or create positive community perception of and/or support for the organization
MARKET POTENTIAL (Demand)	
User Need	We have evidence of social need and open window of opportunity
User Desire	We have evidence of user interest or evidence or success of similar programs in other communities
Funder Interest	We have evidence of interest, or noticeable trends in grant making or contracts for similar services/products
Market Share	We have evidence of an open market with little competition
SUSTAINABILITY POTENTIAL (Capital needs)	
Concept Development	Research and development resources are available or easily accessible
Start up	Low cost of startup and/or easily accessible funding for startup
Cost-to-benefit ratio	Low total program costs compared against high public benefit
Personnel Capacity	Board, faculty, staff, or volunteers capacity is present and aligned with potential service/product
Income Potential	Target population with discretionary income potential and/or evidence of ability to pay fees
Organizational Capacity	Internal structures, space, technology, etc. are in order or easily adjusted for new program or expansion
Funder Interest	Trends or other evidence of funder interest for three-to five-year horizon

123

Starting a New Degree Program is the Last Thing a Dean Should Do

When a school discovers a declining trend in enrollment it's time to huddle for some frantic strategic planning. If anxiety about the enrollment numbers is high enough some will want to talk about how the times they are a changin' for higher education---and how little there is to do about it. Others will focus on branding, some will start asking questions about what the admissions staff is doing---and whether it is doing the right things. Others will lament the loss of an idyllic past when classes were full, student housing had a waiting list, entering students could write, FTE was above average, and there were more bodies around the faculty conference table.

Sometimes the conversation turns to vision and mission. That's always a conversation worth having, it can help people focus on the foundational purpose of the shared enterprise all members of the system commit to, from Faculty and staff to administration and Trustees. But in the case of enrollment the challenge is seldom about vision or mission, rather, the remedy often lies in more pragmatic strategies.

For example, when enrollment is flat, or declining, the best potential for increasing overall enrollment is to expand the student body profile by offering a new degree program. A new degree program diversifies a school's offerings and attracts a previously unreached population. However, starting a new degree program is *the last thing a dean should do.*

The *first* thing a dean should do is lead the Faculty, administration, and key staff in a rigorous assessment of the need for a new program and its viability. There is a risk in plunging too quickly into starting a degree program that sounds like a good idea to the school's stakeholders, but may have little value to the potential audience the school imagines is eager to storm the school's registrar's office when the new program is announced.

Here are some actions the dean may want to implement before starting a new degree program:

- Check accreditation standards and requirements to ensure the school can meet what is necessary to receive approval. Assess the potential institutional impact a new degree program will have. Will a new degree program require additional faculty members? Will it require additional support staff?
- Conduct a study that can confirm the viability of a new degree program. Assess the comprehensive impact of a new program on all systems: classroom space, course schedule, faculty teaching load, advising load, scholarships and financial aid, student services, program support, assessment components, recruitment activities (how much will it cost to recruit one new student in the program?), etc. Will creating a new program require that an existing anemic one close in order to not compete with each other?
- Help internal parties guard against self referencing as rationale. Help the stakeholders focus on data and responsible study and interpretation as the basis for decision-making. Similarly, beware of over-enthusiastic interpretation of alumni surveys about satisfaction and about what new degree program they think the school should offer. Alumni are disconnected from the internal factors that must inform the decision, unaware of broader issues impacting the school, and may not really understand what future alumni need from a new degree program. Their frame of reference is the experience of college they have already had.
- Seek or generate the data necessary to make responsible and realistic decision.

- Perform a potential vs. risk assessment audit.
- Assess if the new degree program will align with the current faculty profile. One dilemma is a new degree program that expands the scope of the curriculum may not be supported by the expertise or scholarship of the current faculty members. This may yield resistance from faculty members who do not feel equipped to teach in the proposed program, or, it may require a commitment to reconstitute the faculty---by adding additional faculty members, replacing current faculty, hiring affiliate faculty, or partnering with another institution. This is where the dean will face the challenge of cultural change as opposed to merely programmatic changes.

A new degree program is too complex and costly an enterprise for a "let's try it and see if it flies" approach. If a program does not have the potential to grow over the course of three to five years it is likely not a sound option for the school, regardless of how many may think it a good idea. Can you identify a large enough prospective student body to start and grow the program? Bear in mind that any number of people may respond to a survey saying they'd be "interested" in the program you are thinking of offering, but a very small percentage of those are viable prospects who will commit to the course of study.

Once the dean leads the Faculty and other key offices in a rigorous enough study that yields confidence that a particular degree program is appropriate and viable, then *the last thing you should do is start a new degree program.*

❖

The Dean as Problem-Solver

Two years into my deanship a friend asked how the job was going: "Is it between '10. The best job ever;' or, '6. I'd rather shoot my eye out with a nail gun;' and '1. I'm recommending my worst enemy for this job.'?" I responded that most days, it was a 7: "It's a challenge." Two years into the deanship I was still in the problem-solving stage. Not that problem-solving ever ends for deans. To say it's a challenge is not a bad thing in that I'm the kind of person attracted to challenges and enjoys solving problems. I've discovered that's not true for all deans. The function of resident problem-solver can come as a surprise to entering deans. For one thing, the number and types of problems deans are called upon to solve are myriad:

- **Personnel problems**: even in schools fortunate enough to have a strong HR office, the dean will be involved in sensitive, complex, and often messy personnel issues. One dean said, "I was surprised by the number of hours I need to spend with the university lawyer over personnel and employment issues."
- **Motivational:** given the pressure points schools are facing (deans will often be called upon to be the voice for a hopeful future, an encourager, a cheerleader, and to set the tone for a positive work environment.
- **Administrative:** allocation of resources, balancing schedules and budgets, granting favor, saying, "No" (or "Maybe later."), are day to day concerns. While Presidents set institutional vision and direction, deans become stewards of strategies and resources. Deans are implementers, they function more like lieutenants than generals.
- **Academic:** this category underscores that deans are *educational* leaders. They must solve problems related to degree standards; curricular review, assessment, and

revision; educational effectiveness; teaching performances; academic probation; accreditation compliance, achieving curricular integration, etc. Of all the institutional problems at the school, this one more than any belongs to the dean.
- **Organizational:** I contend that schools are chronically anxious organizations. They are structured for it. Consequently, schools are organized to resist change (ironic in an educational institution, but, that is its organizational nature). The major problem deans solve organizationally is figuring out how to push against inertia.

The kinds of problems deans solve is one thing, *how* to solve those problems is another. All schools in higher education have the same problems, to one extent or another. This is because schools are systems of a kind with problems endemic to that system. However, each dean must solve his or her own problems for his situation and her context. That is a product of context, personality and capacity, as well as imagination, hard thinking, and sometimes, force of will. It's why it matters that *you* are the dean.

Here are some hints as to how to solve problems:

- There rarely is a perfect solution to a problem. Sometimes, you just need to make a decision; sometimes just making a decision is the solution to a problem. Often, as dean, it's *your* job to make the decision--just do so.
- Think long-term when solving a problem. What is expedient is not always effective in the long run.
- Never underestimate the power of the baser motivations. Fear, greed, self-preservation, pain-avoidance, revenge, often feed the nature of a problem. Use them to solve the impasse.
- For some things, a higher level of incentives yields lower performance. This seems to be especially true with Faculty.

Find out what really motivates your faculty members (hint: it's usually not higher salaries).
- Try to solve a problem once. When I served on a key committee at my former school I discovered that the committee was solving the same problem over and over. When I became dean I resolved to "fix" as many problems only once. That's where a policy manual becomes a godsend and not a burden. When a problem arose, we determined the best solution, and if appropriate drafted either a policy or a procedure for the next time the problem arose.
- If you can't immediately change the problem, change yourself. Albert Einstein said "You cannot solve a problem with the same mind that created it." Often a solution to the problem happens when we change our thinking, or, we change the way we feel about it.
- When solving a problem, solve the actual problem. It's worth the time to discern what the problem actually is. As my engineer son says, "Solve the *problem*, not something else." Good advice.
- Discern if the problem is your problem. Deans are "convenient" and often are asked to solve other people's problems. If the problem belongs to someone else, don't over function---allow others the joy of solving their own problems.
- Accept that not all problems need to be solved. Sometimes, problems serve a purpose in chronically anxious system. Solving one problem sometimes just creates another three.

Schools in higher education are caught in the perfect storm of change: an economic model that is no longer viable; the fast-paced fundamental changes in the field of education; the upheaval in the landscape of culture and society). That means deans will always have problems to solve. And while some problems are unsolvable, deans will be called to address those nevertheless. I'm of the opinion the schools that will survive will be those fleet enough to change and morph their models and forms while maintaining their identity and mission. That's no small feat, one that will require imagination and courage in solving, or redefining, our problems. Deans, of course, will be at the center of it all.

❖

The Dean and Wicked Problems

One of the most critical skills academic deans need, arguably now more than ever before, is that of problem solving. The challenges facing schools continue to become more technologically complex, socially entangled, costly, and multi-faceted. It is evident that most deans are not just dealing with programmatic, administrative, and technological problems, they are dealing with *wicked problems.* The experience can feel like trying to unravel an endless Gordian knot.

A wicked problem is a form of social or cultural problem that is difficult to solve because of incomplete, contradictory, and changing requirements for their solution. When these problems are unrecognized as such the attempt is to solve them through policies, the wrong means, or, simply ignored as too hard to tackle, merely kicking the proverbial can down the road, only to have it come back worse.

Horst Rittel, one of the first to research wicked problems, references ten characteristics that describe this sort of complicated challenge:

Wicked problems have no definitive formulation. Therefore, it becomes difficult for a dean to define the problem that needs to be addressed. This is a significant challenge given the tendency for people to want to know the *one* answer and simplest solution to a complex problem. With complex problems, it's never about just one thing.

Wicked problems have no stopping rule, or criteria upon which to determine "solving." Unlike challenges with clearly defined outcomes and measures of completion, wicked problems are persistent and tend to be moving targets. The answer to "When will we ever solve this problem?" is "Never."

Solutions to wicked problems are not true or false; they can only be good or bad. When deans tackle wicked problems the best approach is to choose the best strategy at the time. Arguing about what "should" or "should not" be is pointless.

There is no complete list of applicable "moves" for a solution to a wicked problem. Wicked problems require deans to be imaginative, fleet, flexible, and innovative.

There are always more than one explanation for a wicked problem, with the appropriateness of the explanation depending on the individual perspective of the perceiver. Hence, deans will constantly deal with the impasse of multiple interpretations. The President will see it one way, the Faculty another, Trustees in their own way, donors and students differently altogether. Where one sits in the system determines one's perspective. It should come as no surprise, then, that no one will see the problem in the same way the dean does. This requires a multi-disciplinary approach to most wicked problems, as no singular perspective suffices.

Every wicked problem is a symptom of another problem. Like a knotted bunch of cords, pulling on one end of the problem merely creates tension and tightens the knot on the other end. Deans need to be systems thinkers, understanding the interconnected complexity of the enterprise.

No solution of a wicked problem has a definitive, scientific test. When proposing strategies for addressing complex problems deans often face the call to give evidence or proof that the action will be successful. That's just not possible with wicked problems. They require the courage to risk and the ability to adapt along the way.

Every wicked problem is unique. The problems facing colleges and universities in higher education are endemic to all schools merely by virtue that they are systems of a type. But it remains true that each dean will have to solve their own problems in their own context.

Finally, to paraphrase Rittel, **deans attempting to solve a wicked problem must be fully responsible for their actions.** That's the burden of leadership. Few, if any, in the organization will take responsibility for tackling wicked problems. That comes with the job of being the dean.[1]

While not all problems a dean faces are wicked, those that are will be the most demanding. Even difficult problems can have a solution, and most deans can get adept at tackling them. But wicked problems will be the most challenging to educational leaders due to the indeterminate scope and scale required to address them. Wicked problems can't be fixed; they'll be the bane of every successive dean and President in office.

- What are the wicked problems you face in your school?
- Who are you consulting with on addressing the wicked problems?
- Are you aware of your biases which may hinder you from seeing alternative and imaginative approaches?
- Are you alert to unintended consequences as you apply strategies to wicked problems?

[1] See Jean-Pierre Protzen and David J. Harris, *The Universe of Design: Horst Rittel's Theories of Design and Planning* (Routledge, 2010).

Six Types of Assessment Every Dean Needs to Use

Persons new to the office of the Dean may soon discover the need to acquire a new set of skills to effectively carry out the job. Those skills range from supervision, emotional support (yes, more than you imagined!), educational administrative planning, curriculum design and planning, political acumen, budgeting and financial management, and assessment. Of these, none seems to puzzle novice deans more than educational assessment. While it can seem daunting, as I sometimes tell deans asking for help in this practice, "It's not rocket science, but it helps if you know what you're doing."

There are six types of assessment practices, which, used together, will provide the dean a multifaceted and holistic view of student learning outcomes and program effectiveness. These will provide deans, and Faculty, the data needed to evaluate the effectiveness of the curricula and to make wise and appropriate adjustments. Good data, rigorously derived, make for better decision-making than hunches, good-sounding ideas, predilections, or fads. As well, these assessments will provide the information needed to demonstrate rigorous academic practices to accrediting bodies.

The Six Types of Assessments

DIAGNOSTIC

Diagnostic assessment measures a student's, or a class of students', strengths, weaknesses, knowledge, and skills prior to an instructional set (a course), or prior to starting a program of study. Examples of diagnostic assessments used in schools include the Test of English as a Foreign Language (TOEFL), a language proficiency exam given to international applicants, and the Graduate Record Exam (GRE). Some schools may administer writing assessments to evaluate the need for remedial work in preparation for academic writing in a degree program. Some programs use the Graduate Management Admissions Test (GMAT) as part of their admissions requirements. Some schools administered the Minnesota Multiphasic Personality Inventory (MMPI-2-RF) a standardized psychometric test of adult personality and psychopathology, as part of their application process.

FORMATIVE

Formative assessment practices give evidence of a student's performance during instruction, during a learning experience, or in the midst of a course of study. Formative assessments are applied regularly at intervals throughout the instruction process. An example is a multi-faceted "mid-course" assessment with a faculty adviser to review academic performance and progress through a degree program course of study. This can include a student's self-assessment about their progress in formation goals. For students, formative assessments is an opportunity to receive feedback on academic performance and other goals.

SUMMATIVE

Summative evaluations measure a student's achievement at the conclusion of an instructional set or course of study. The most obvious course level summative assessment are final exams and the final grade a student receives in a course. At the program level, summative assessments can include a grade distribution analysis, program retention and completion rates, graduating class profiles, and, a grade point analysis of graduating students (highest, lowest, median, average).

NORM-REFERENCED

Norm-referenced, sometimes commonly called "standardized" tests, compares a student's performance against a national or other "norm" group. Examples of norm-referenced tests include the SAT, IQ tests, and tests that are graded on a curve offering a percentile rank. Due to the loose and broad interpretation of accreditation standards, the wide variety of school cultures and contexts, and the range and amorphous nature of what constitutes achievement and competencies, norm-referenced assessments can be subjective in their application and interpretations.

CRITERION-REFERENCED

This assessment practice measures a student's performance against a published goal, specific objectives, or standards. The most common criteria are interpretations of accreditation or states standards (e.g., Common Core) in program goals and the derivative student learning outcomes embedded in courses and program components. The application of well-designed assessment rubrics aid in the assessment of criterion-referenced evaluations.

BENCHMARK

Benchmark evaluations are similar to some of the above. These practices are used to evaluate student performance at periodic intervals, or at the end of a grading period. They can be used to predict student performance on end-of-course summative tests, or, end-of-program competencies evaluations. Benchmark evaluations can also be used to predict student performance post-graduation. The use of alumni surveys evaluated with alignment with degree program goals can help in benchmark assessment. Again, the range ministry contexts in which alumni serve, and the amorphous nature of what constitutes achievement and competencies, provide a challenge for schools to establish benchmarks. The increasing attention to competency-based programs will likely require schools to identify "benchmarks" as indicators of levels of competencies.

- How many of these six assessments do you apply in your evaluation practices in your school?
- Which might you need to implement to provide a richer and more balanced assessment profile for your school?
- How, for whom, and where will you publish the results of your assessments? For information? For accountability? For reporting?

❖

Using Grade Distribution Reports

Grades have always been an anxiety-causing practice--something I've personally witnessed as an elementary school principle and a graduate school dean (once receiving a phone call from the mother who wanted to challenge the grade given to her graduate school son!). Few charges against higher education, or a school, however, are as cringe-worthy as that of engaging in "grade inflation." That's justifiable on many levels. At heart grades are less a reflection of a professor's acuity, than an indication of how well the students learned.

Grades may be seen as everything from a necessary evil to a responsible pedagogical practice. On the positive side, using grades for assessing the effectiveness of a program of study can help the dean, and Faculty answer important questions:

- How well have students, as a class or cohort, realized the course learning outcomes?
- To what extent and how well can the student demonstrate mastery of knowledge and skill?

- How does one class compare to another comparable class in student learning achievement?
- How have students performed over time when comparing grades?
- Can grades reveal how effective assessment tools are in evaluating student learning?
- Are instructors consistent in how they assess student learning?
- Do grades reflect changes made to the curriculum? Its content or learning methods?
- Do grades help interpret the learning experience and achievements of particular student profiles?
- How do grades impact the GPA profile of students by cohorts, entering class, particular student profiles?
- Do grades reveal a bias toward or against certain student profiles (gender, race, culture, socio-economic)?
- Is there evidence of grade inflation?

Disseminating the analysis of student grades can help faculty identify and explore challenges and issues related to student learning. In addition to providing the general grades report, the dean may present a comparative profile on the grade distribution by: (a) comparison of students who work more than 20 hours per week; (b) by gender; (3) by ethnic profile; (4) by commuters verses residential; (5) by age profile. In addition publishing a three-year comparison of grade distributions can help identify trends and their cause.

Validity in Comparisons

It is important that grading be consistent across courses in a program of study. The validity of the assessment, and fairness to students and constituents, necessitates there be consistent grading practices and means of evaluation among courses of the same level. A more accurate profile of grade distribution can be achieved by analyzing grades by course levels:

- Introductory and survey courses: open to first-year students; lacking prerequisites.
- Intermediate courses: generally not open to first-year students and requiring prerequisite(s).
- Advanced course: ordinarily for students earning a major, in a concentration, or certificate. These courses tend to require prior knowledge or prerequisites and focus on a particular topic or specific area of knowledge within a discipline.
- Independent studies, tutorials, projects, etc.

Resources for grading practices

While grading can often be more intuitive than rigorously-calculated in some cases, instructors must strive to accurately assess student learning achievement. For both instructors and students, providing objective measures for assessment of learning can promote better grading and learning. For example, both students and faculty should make use of standardized measures such as:

- Grading scale with qualitative description
- Program-level rubrics
- Course-level rubrics
- A standardized grades calculator.

As with all program level assessment practices, a grade distribution analysis and report should lead to decisions about implementation.

❖

Using Program-Level Assessment Rubrics

Using program-level assessment rubrics for direct assessment provides the ability to evaluate the quality of student learning outcomes across the span of the curricular program of study. Applying a program-level rubric will provide a more uniform and standardized understanding of student achievement in the curriculum. While individual courses may use instructor-designed rubrics for individual courses, the program-level rubrics can help integrate evidence of learning in student work across the curriculum. The rubrics can also help faculty members sharpen their own individual course rubrics as they compare them to a standard. Further, instructors can align the student assignments rubrics in their courses with the program level rubrics. A standardized critical evaluation of student work provides a more accurate measure of student learning than indirect assessment methods.

As a case study, in one school the Faculty identified four common types of student work used throughout the curriculum (they discovered this using a curriculum map). Most course assignments in the curriculum fell under one of the four types of student-produced work.

Once the Faculty identified the four categories of student work, it was able to create program-level rubrics for each type. Creating one rubric for each "type" of student work is more efficient than trying to manage multiple individual instructor-created rubrics from assignments in courses across the curriculum. Once the rubrics were produced, the Faculty was also able to use embedded learning outcomes based on the rubrics in every individual course. Embedded learning outcomes helped ensure integration in the course of study (the curriculum), and provided the ability to apply a more standardized metric for student performance throughout the curriculum.

THE FOUR TYPES OF STUDENT WORK

1. Reflection papers.

In these student learning products students are required to demonstrate skill and capacity in critical reflection by: (1) demonstrating personal reflection related to concepts; (2) demonstrating self-understanding related to identity and experience; and (3) reflecting on praxis experiences as a way to derive meaningful learning and insights about competency in practice and to identify areas for improvement.

2. Interpretation papers and products.

In these products students are required to demonstrate skill and understanding in the application of interpretation by: (1) interpreting texts; (2) interpreting professional work contexts; (3) interpreting and integrating academic cognate area discipline specific skills, ethos, and knowledge.

3. Academic research papers and products.

In these products students are required to demonstrate skill and understanding in the application of academic research skills by the producing rigorous academic research papers such as journal articles, monographs, exegetical papers, essays, and book projects.

4. Performance and praxis products.

In these products students are required to give evidence of skill attainment and competence in the application of knowledge through demonstration, practice, or performance. Performance can take many forms and may use a variety of media: live classroom or studio performance, lecture or teaching a class in context, internship, graphic and media arts products, performance in practicum courses or seminars, etc. For this student product the school may collect and archive recordings of performances, but will need also to collect narrative assessment reports of such performances.

USING PROGRAM-LEVEL ASSESSMENT RUBRICS

For the purpose of assessing degree program-level learning outcomes the school uses the four rubrics and applies them to each type of student work product. The four assessment rubrics identify course-embedded general program learning outcomes and provide a standardized interpretive qualitative scoring scale. The general program level assessment rubrics are applied at the conclusion of every academic year. The evaluative comments from the rubrics, as well as the quantitative summary, become the source of an evaluation report. The report, in turn, becomes the basis for refinement in teaching-learning strategies and curriculum design as needed.

Below are templates for each of the student product types. You can use this as a starting point for creating your own program level assessment rubrics.

1. Reflection Learning Outcomes Assessment Rubric

1. Reflection Student Learning Products	
Student product examples	*Description of learning intent or outcome*
Concept or theory reflection paper Case study Reflection paper Autobiographies Student essays Growth plans	The student will be able to… ☐ identify personal strengths and weaknesses as teacher, communicator, community leader, etc. ☐ assess values held and expressed by others from individual, cultural, social familial, and global perspectives ☐ use a conceptual construct or concepts for naming, explaining, and interpreting experiences ☐ provide interpretation of meaning to personal experience ☐ use values and standards of judgment from different disciplines ☐ distinguish among personal, ethical, aesthetic, cultural, secular, and religious values ☐ identify values expressed in feelings, attitudes, beliefs, choices and commitments ☐ distinguish among personal, ethical, aesthetic, cultural, secular, and religious values ☐ employ values and standards of judgment informed by academic disciplines ☐ articulate a considered and self-determined sense of agency and personal values

2. Interpretation Learning Outcomes Assessment Rubric

2. Interpretation Student Learning Products	
Student product	*Description of learning intent or outcome*
Textual exegetical paper Literary interpretation paper Student lectures Case study Organizational assessment project Philosophy interpretation essays Verbatims Exam essay	The student will be able to... ☐ accurately explain or translate data, information, concepts and principles ☐ accurately extrapolate conclusions and implications from data ☐ appropriately use different mediums to interpret data, concepts, information, and principles ☐ interpret concepts, data, information, and principles to target audience appropriately and effectively ☐ appropriately explicate or translate the meaning and implications of data, information, concepts, and principles ☐ can both use media effectively and appropriately as well as effectively evidence interpretation ☐ identify meaning and relationships among the objects or focus of study (e.g., text, audience, context)

3. Academic Learning Outcomes Assessment Rubric

3. Academic research Products	
Student product	*Description of learning intent or outcome*
Academic research paper Essay Textual exegesis paper Independent studies Theses	The student will be able to… ☐ identify data, ideas, patterns, principles, concepts, perspectives correctly ☐ use facts, formulas, concepts, procedures appropriately and correctly ☐ draw appropriate and accurate conclusions ☐ integrate ideas and values from different discipline areas ☐ revise conclusions in light of new insights, observation, interpretations, information, or reasoning ☐ choose appropriate communication mode and media for purpose and occasion ☐ draw valid conclusions ☐ revise conclusions and beliefs consistent with new learning, interpretations, or reasoning. ☐ apply and use standard academic research format correctly (Chicago, Turabian, MLA) ☐ use correct use of grammar, syntax, style & form in academic writing

4. Performance Learning Outcomes Assessment rubric.

4. Performance and Praxis Products	
Student product	*Description of learning intent or outcome*
Student sermons Faith interviews Student sermons Supervisor report weekly visitation practicum Designing worship Services Supervisor report	The student will be able to… ☐ apply disciplinary knowledge, skills, and value to professional or academic context ☐ implement effective problem-solving, discernment, and decision making strategies ☐ perform effectively and appropriately in work setting or academic context ☐ demonstrate practical application of theory, concepts, or principles ☐ demonstrate capacity for innovation and interpretation of skills acquisition and application ☐ respond appropriately to challenging and changing work contexts in behavior and intervention actions ☐ act and perform effectively and appropriately in different contexts and settings ☐ demonstrate a high level of performance which reflect discipline standards

Appendix

13 Noteworthy Quotes from 13 Deans

Management is easy, leadership is hard. Most school deans can get up to speed on educational program management in relatively short order. It takes about three to four years to learn the finer aspects of the job, but, given the press of the immediate, effective deans get good, real fast, about attending to the nuts and bolts of management and supervision. Fortunately, most organizations can carry on, pushed by momentum, until atrophy requires the new dean to start pushing against inertia, or, to assess and question ineffective and outmoded ways of doing the routine. At some point during the second year, a new dean will likely ask, "Why do we do it that way?" To which the answer will likely be, "I don't know. We've always done it that way."

In the midst of attending to the necessary, two larger issues loom in the foreground for many deans: vocation and leadership. Here are thirteen noteworthy quotes from thirteen experienced deans on the larger questions of vocation and leadership:

On Vocation

1. "Nothing is irrelevant to our vocation. We may have what feel like 'hidden years,' spent on apparently disconnected activities and 'details' without any great sense of integrating purpose, only to find later that the quality of those details has been crucial for fulfilling a life's work." David F. Ford. Quoted in "The Vocation of the Academic Dean," by Stephen R. Graham, in *C(H)AOS Theory: Reflections of Chief Academic Officers in Theological Education*, p. 67.

2. "The shift from serving primarily as a teacher to serving primarily as an administrator is not a change of vocation, but a change within a vocation. The academic vocation is rich in the options it holds. Administration is not a sell-out or a loss of that vocation, but simply another way of responding to the call to the academic life and service of the theological school community." Jeanne McLean, "The Study of Chief Academic Officers in Theological Schools : Reflections on Academic Leadership," *Theological Education* 33 Aug 1996, Suppl, p 1-76.

3. "There are at least four kinds of people who should not become chief academic officers: those who are happiest among stacks of books and at classroom lecterns; those who relist the satisfying sense of work completed; those who thrive on calm and predictability in their daily routines; those who agonize fiercely over conflict and criticism. Being an administrator is neither more nor less difficult than being a professor. It is, however, different." Elizabeth C. Nordbeck, "The Once and Future Dean: Reflections of Being a Chief Academic Officer," *Theological Education* vol. 33, Supplement, (1996): 21-23.

4. "The vantage point of the academic dean is different from that of a faculty member. Even though you share in the same core activities that define the work of a faculty member--teaching, research, service, community life---as CAO you see the world of your institution differently than does your colleague down the hall." Gail R. O'Day, "Stop, Look, and Listen: Observation in Academic Leadership," in *C(H)AOS Theory: Reflections of Chief Academic Officers in Theological Education.*

5. "...what it means to serve in the capacity of CAO—to respond to the call of God. To fill this role is a calling, an assignment, a divine appointment that the CAO may not immediately perceive. The vocational call is sensitive to self calling self to a place of ministry. Self must agree with God's call before self can call self to ministry." Linda W. Bryan, "The Vocational Call and Multiple

Occupations of a CA)," in *C(H)AOS Theory: Reflections of Chief Academic Officers in Theological Education.*

6. The factors that cause stress and the difficult challenges about which academic officers speak are explicit, clearly defined, and quite concrete. The rewards, on the other hand, are subtle, uncertain, and more elusive in nature. They have to do with making meaning in the life and vocation of the academic officer." Karen M. Ristau, "Challenged of Academic Administration: Rewards and Stresses in the Role of the Chief Academic Officer." *Academic Leadership: A Study of Academic Officers in Theological Schools. Monographs on Academic Leadership.* March 1996.

On Leadership

7. "Right now, . . . schools need leaders, not just managers. The church has changed and is changing, the world has changed and will continue to change, and the persons serving in many theological schools actively resist the changes that might be necessary for them to serve faithfully in this new context, or, in some cases, even to survive." Stephen R. Graham, "The Vocation of the Academic Dean," in *C(H)AOS Theory: Reflections of Chief Academic Officers in Theological Education.*

8. "Working in and through change is perhaps one of the most significant and essential roles the dean plays in governance. The manner in which the dean understands and manages resistance must ultimately lead toward a communal appreciation for the implications of continued resistance for the mission of the institution as well as its faculty, students, and staff." Anne T. Anderson, "Fulcrum Leadership and the Varied Dimensions of Governance," in *C(H)AOS Theory: Reflections of Chief Academic Officers in Theological Education.*

9. "I developed a theory as dean that the faculty, students, and president spent much of the weekend thinking up things to tell

the dean on Monday morning about what was wrong with the institution, or the curriculum, or the student body or, heaven forbid, the current dean. .... Monday ... remained the day when crimes of passion were confessed, revolutionary new utopias were set forth and unexpected insights into the will of God were duly reported." Wilson Yates, "The Art and Politics of Deaning," *Theological Education,* Volume 34, Number 1 (1997): 85-96.<p>

10. "A tension that is quite pronounced within all of higher education is the inherent friction between a school's need for a common understanding of its mission and the tendency of scholarly training to enhance individualism." Sale R. Stoffer, "Faculty Leadership and Development," in *C(H)AOS Theory: Reflections of Chief Academic Officers in Theological Education.*

11. "Alignment with ethos is the most important consideration when building or winnowing the faculty. Academic, scholarly, and ministerial qualifications for appointment to the faculty must be honoured, but never at the expense of alignment with the institution's ethos." Robert W. Ferris, "The Work of a Dean." *Evangelical Review of Theology* (2008) 32:1, 65-73.

12. "Deans have commented, not entirely in jest, that the job requires the intellectual breadth of Leonardo, the communication skill of Dale Carnegie, and the fortitude of Attila the Hun. Rare is the person who takes on an academic leadership position fully prepared. . . . . deans learn principally 'on the job.'" Jeanne P. McLean, "Professional Development for Chief Academic Officers." *Academic Leadership: A Study of Academic Officers in Theological Schools Monographs on Academic Leadership.* November 1996.

13. "The president is guardian of the institutional ethos, but the dean's hands hold the levers by which ethos is conveyed to the next generation, magnified or diminished." Robert W. Ferris, "The Work of a Dean." *Evangelical Review of Theology* (2008) 32:1, 65-73.

Bibliography

Alexander, John B.; Groller, Richard and Morris Janet. *The Warrior's Edge: Frontline Strategies for Victory on the Corporate Battlefield.* New York: Avon Books, 1990.

Allen, Mary. *Assessing Academic Programs in Higher Education.* Jossey-Bass, 2003.

Banta, Trudy, Elizabeth A.Jones, and Karen E. Black, *Designing Effective Assessment: Principles and Profiles of Good Practice.* Jossey-Bass, 2009.

Bergquist, William H. *Engaging the Six Cultures of the Academy.* Jossey-Bass, 2007.

Bolman, Lee G. and Joan V. Gallos. *Reframing Academic Leadership.* Jossey-Bass, 2011.

Brent, Ruben. *A Guide for Leaders in Higher Education: Core Concepts, Competencies, and Tools.* Stylus Publishing, 2016.

Buller, Jeffrey L. *The Essential Academic Dean or Provost.* Jossey-Bass, 2015.

Caplow, Theodore. *How To Run Any Organization.* New York: The Dryden Press, 1976.

Champlin, John Rice, "A study and analysis of the utilization and influence of the critical factors of change in the schools of Concord, Massachusetts, 1965-1970." (1971). *Doctoral Dissertations 1896 - February 2014. 2510.*

Cialdini, *Influence: The Psychology of Persuasion.* Harper Business, 2006.

Cloud, Henry. *Boundaries for Leaders: Results, Relationships, and being Ridiculously in Charge.* Harper Business, 2013.

Davis, James R. *Learning to Lead: A Handbook for Postsecondary Administrators.* Rowen & Littlefield, 2011.

Denning, Stephen. *The Leader's Guide to Radical Management: Reinventing the Workplace for the 21st Century.* Jossey-Bass, 2010.

Drake, Susan. *Creating Standards-Based Integrated Curriculum: The Common Core States Standards Edition.* Corwin, 2012.

Edwards, Betty. *Drawing on the Right Side of the Brain.* Los Angeles, California: J.P. Tarcher, 1989.

Fisher and Ury, *Getting to Yes.* Penguin Books, 2011.

Friedman, Edwin H. *A Failure of Nerve.* New York: Seabury Books, 2007.

Galindo, Israel. *A Guide to Online Course Design and Instruction.* Educational Consultants, 2016.

Grogan, Margaret (ed), *The Jossey-Bass Reader on Educational Leadership.* Jossey-Bass, 2013.

Hill and Lineback, *Being the Boss: The 3 Imperatives for Becoming a Great Leader.* Harvard Business Review Press, 2019.

Kouzes, James M. *The Jossey-Bass Administrator's Guide to Exemplary Leadership.* Jossey-Bass, 2003.

Kuh, George D. Association of American Colleges and Universities, "High-Impact Educational Practices: What they are, who has access to them, and why they matter." You can order a copy of the report from www.aacu.org

Laufgraben, Jodi Levine and Nancy S. Shapiro. *Sustaining and Improving Learning Communities.* Jossey-Bass, 2004.

Lick, Dale W. "Leadership and Change," in R. M. Diamond, ed. *Field Guide to Academic Leadership.* A publication of the National Academy for Academic Leadership. Jossey-Bass, 2002.

Lucas, Ann. *Leading Academic Change: Essential Roles for Department Chairs.* Jossey-Bass, 2000.

Ludvik, Marilee J. Bresciani and Ralph Wolff. *Outcomes-Based Academic and Co-Curricular Program Review: A Compilation of Institutional Good Practice.* Stylus Publishing, 2006.

Machiavelli, *The Prince.* Available from various publishers.

Marcuson, Margaret. *Leaders Who Last: Sustaining Yourself and Your Ministry.* Seabury Books, 2009.

McLean, Jeanne P. *Leading From the Center : The Emerging Role of the Chief Academic Officer in Theological Schools.* Scholars Press, 1999.

Oshry, Berry. *Seeing Systems: Unlocking the Mysteries of Organizational Life.* San Francisco: Berrett-Koehler Publishers, 2007.

Protzen, Jean-Pierre and David J. Harris, *The Universe of Design: Horst Rittel's Theories of Design and Planning.* Routledge, 2010.

Roper, Susan and Terrance Deal. *Peak performance for Deans and Chairs.* Rowan & Littlefield, 2010.

Schon, Donald A. *The Reflective Practitioner: How Professionals Think in Action.* Basic Books Inc., 1983.

Simon, Herbert. *The Sciences of the Artificial.* Cambridge, Mass.: MIT Press, 1972.

Small, Kyle J. A. "Successful Leadership in the Early Years of Ministry: Reflections for Leadership Formation in Theological Education," *Journal of Religious Leadership* (vol. 10, no. 1, spring 2011).

Spreitzer, Gretchen M. and Scott Sonenschein, "Toward the Construct Definition of Positive Deviance," *American Behavioral Scientist.* Vol. 47, Issue 6. February 2004.

Stone, et al., *Difficult Conversations: How to Discuss What Matters Most.* Penguin Books 2010.

Suskie, Linda. *Assessing Student Learning: A Common Sense Guide.* Jossey-Bass, 2018.

Turak, August. "The 11 Leadership Secrets You've Never Heard About." Available at: https://www.forbes.com/sites/augustturak/2012/07/17/the-11-leadership-secrets-you-never-heard-about/#59092b2119f4

Ury, *Getting Past No: Negotiating in Difficult Situations.* Bantam, 1993.

Walvoord, Barbara E. and Trudy W. Banta. *Assessment Clear and Simple: A Practical Guide for Institutions, Departments, and General Education.* Jossey-Bass, 2010.

Made in the USA
Monee, IL
14 July 2021